WHISPERS OF THE HEART

*Journeys with the Prayers
of Imam Zayn al-Abidin (AS)*

ABBAS SADAK

Whispers of the Heart – Journeys with the prayers of Imam Zayn-Al-Abidin (AS)
Written by Abbas Sadak
Copyright © 2025 Abbas Sadak

All rights reserved. No part of this publication may be reproduced, distributed, or transmitted in any form or by any means, including photocopying, recording, or other electronic or mechanical methods, without the prior written permission of the publisher, except in the case of brief quotations embodied in reviews or academic research.

For permissions, feedback or inquiries, contact:
Abbas Sadak
Email: abbassadak@aol.com

Published By Abbas Sadak
First Edition: December 2025

ISBN: 978-1-0683208-9-7 (Paperback)
ISBN: 978-1-9193799-0-6 (E-Book)

This book is a work of devotion and historical reflection. While every effort has been made to ensure the accuracy of the information, the author and publisher disclaim any liability for errors or omissions.

All proceeds from this book will be used to support charitable initiatives.

Disclaimer:

The material has been reviewed and validated by scholars. May Allah reward them for their time and guidance. Any mistakes or shortcomings are the author's alone, and forgiveness is humbly sought from Allah and the readers.

All Quranic verses, narrations, and historical references are used with respect and reverence.

Contents Page

Dedication..i

Introduction – The Voice that Survived...........................iii

Preface – The book of whispers and the book of light.....vii

Authors Note..xi

Chapter 1 — The Call to Awareness...............................1

Chapter 2 — The Mirror of the Soul..............................9

Chapter 3 — The Weight of Wrong................................15

Chapter 4 — The Quiet Battle...................................21

Chapter 5 — The Gift of Gratitude..............................27

Chapter 6 — The Bonds That Raised Me...........................33

Chapter 7 — Circles of Trust...................................39

Chapter 8 — Lessons and Learning...............................45

Chapter 9 — Earning and Enoughness.............................51

Chapter 10 — Body and Breath...................................57

Chapter 11 — The Voice of Service..............................63

Chapter 12 — Purpose and Path..................................69

Chapter 13 — Justice and Responsibility........................75

Chapter 14 — Leadership and Trust..............................81

Chapter 15 — Nature and the Elements...........................87

Chapter 16 — Time and Turning Points...........................93

Chapter 17 — The Heart That Loves..............................99

Chapter 18 — Hope and Doubt......................105

Chapter 19 — The World and Creation...........111

Chapter 20 — The Beauty of Worship............117

Chapter 21 — The Traveller's Path................123

Chapter 22 — The Power of Words...............129

Chapter 23 — The Lantern of Learning..........135

Chapter 24 — The Return............................141

GLOSSARY..147

EPILOGUE — THE CIRCLE OF LIGHT............149

ACKNOWLEDGEMENTS..................................155

INDEX OF DUAS REFERENCED IN THIS BOOK.............157

DEDICATION

For the seekers of silence
who still believe that whispers reach Heaven.

For every heart that bends but does not break,
every soul learning to speak to its Creator again.

For the youth who wonder if faith can feel real —
may these pages show that it can,
and that the Divine has always been listening.

INTRODUCTION — THE VOICE THAT SURVIVED

There are moments in history when words are all that remain, when kingdoms fall, voices are silenced, and yet one whisper outlives the noise.

The Sahīfa al-Kāmilah al-Sajjādiyyah is one of those whispers.

It is not only a book of supplications — it is a survival of the soul.

Its author, **Imam Zayn al- ʿĀbidīn (A.S)**, lived in the shadow of **Karbala**, the most searing tragedy in Islamic memory.

He was the great-grandson of the Prophet Muhammad ﷺ,

the son of Imam al-Husayn عليه السلام —and one of the few who survived the massacre that claimed his family and companions.

He witnessed horror beyond what words can hold.

He was chained, humiliated, and paraded through the streets of Kufa and Damascus —a prisoner of conscience, too weak to fight but too faithful to yield.

And yet, when he was finally freed, he did not rebuild with swords.

He rebuilt with supplications.

A Life Written in Whispers

Imam Zayn al-ʿĀbidīn (A.S) spoke softly, but his words carried galaxies.

Through his prayers, he re-taught a broken community how to feel again —how to pray, how to forgive, how to hope.

Where fear silenced tongues, he gave people words to speak to God.

Where trauma hardened hearts, he softened them with remembrance.

His Sahīfa — meaning "record" or "scroll" — was more than a collection of prayers.

It was a reconstruction of faith.

Each du'ā' rebuilt a moral world that had been shattered by tyranny.

He spoke about justice and humility, about the rights of parents and neighbours, about patience, gratitude, and knowledge. He spoke about illness and healing, sin and mercy, time and death.

But he spoke always in the language of love.

Even when he wept, his tears were prayers.

Even when he grieved, his grief became gratitude.

That is why the Sahīfa still feels alive — because it was born not from theory, but from experience that touched both heaven and earth.

The Heart of the Sahīfa

At its essence, the Sahīfa al-Sajjādiyyah is a bridge between the human and the Divine.

It shows that spirituality is not the denial of emotion — it is the sanctification of it.

It does not demand perfection, but presence. It meets the believer in weakness and teaches that even fragility can be worship.

In it, the Imam turns everything into conversation: fear into prayer, pain into poetry, love into remembrance.

His duʿās are filled with contrasts — majestic yet intimate, sorrowful yet serene. They remind us that faith is not always loud; sometimes it whispers.

To read the Sahīfa is to learn how to speak honestly to God — without pretense, without formula, without shame.

It is a text that teaches the art of spiritual authenticity.

Why It Matters Now

We live in an age of noise — constant messages, endless comparisons, unspoken loneliness. And yet, within that noise, the soul still aches for stillness. It still asks the same questions the Imam once answered:

What does it mean to trust when life feels uncertain? How do I find purpose when I feel unseen? How do I stay kind in a world that glorifies ego?

The Sahīfa does not lecture. It listens.It holds your struggles without judgment, then slowly turns them into prayer.

It reminds you that spirituality is not an escape — it is engagement. That faith is not the absence of questions — it is the courage to ask them with love.

And that prayer, in its truest form, is not about changing God's will, but aligning the heart to it.

The Living Legacy

More than thirteen centuries later, the Sahīfa al-Kāmilah al-Sajjādiyyah remains a companion across generations. It has been studied by scholars, quoted by mystics, and recited by the faithful in every language.

But its real legacy is quieter — in the single tear that falls during its recitation, in the moment someone reads it and whispers, "This is how I feel too."

Through this book, the Imam's voice still travels — from Medina to Damascus, from captivity to freedom, from sorrow to serenity.

And now, into your hands.

A Living Invitation

As you begin this journey through the duʿās, remember: you are not just reading about prayer. You are joining a conversation that never ended.

Let the Imam's voice guide you — not as a teacher standing above, but as a friend walking beside you, reminding you that the path of worship is not far from the path of life.

Every chapter in this book is a step on that path — from awareness to repentance, from gratitude to love, from trust to return.

And somewhere along the way, you may discover that you, too, are capable of speaking to God with the same honesty — the same courage, the same tenderness.

Because that is what the Sahīfa ultimately teaches: that the distance between the human heart and the Divine is only as wide as our remembrance.

"O God," the Imam whispered, "if You were not merciful, who could hope?

And if You were not forgiving, who would dare to speak?"

PREFACE — THE BOOK OF WHISPERS, THE BOOK OF LIGHT

There are books you read, and there are books that read you.

As-Sahīfa al-Kāmilah al-Sajjādiyyah — the collection of supplications by **Imam Zayn al-ʿĀbidīn (A.S)**, the great-grandson of the Prophet ﷺ — belongs to the second kind.

It is not a manual of rituals or a record of rules.

It is the sound of a heart speaking to its Creator — through gratitude, longing, grief, and love.

Across centuries and languages, it has been called "The Psalms of Islam" — a book where every emotion finds a home.

The Imam's duʿās are not distant or abstract; they are human, trembling, and beautifully honest.

They were whispered after tragedy, in the stillness after Karbala, when the world had turned silent — and yet, they shimmer with hope.

This book you now hold is not a translation of the Sahīfa.

It is a journey through it — a map of reflection, written to help readers of all ages, especially the young, walk alongside the Imam's voice.

It is an attempt to bring his prayers into the rhythm of modern life — into the classroom, the home, the late-night scroll, the anxious heart, the quiet morning.

Why This Book Exists

Many of us know what it means to pray, but few of us are taught how to feel while praying.

We are taught the words, but not always the wonder. We repeat the motions, but rarely pause to listen for the echo within.

The Saḥīfa is the bridge between knowing and feeling — between form and meaning. It transforms prayer from an act into a relationship.

In these pages, each duʿāʾ has been reimagined not as a historical text, but as a conversation — between you and the Divine, between your present and your purpose. Every section is built around a central theme: patience, gratitude, love, justice, trust, knowledge, and return. Each draws directly from the Saḥīfa's original words, then expands into story, reflection, and modern language.

It is not a replacement for the Imam's words. It is a pathway toward them — a way to feel what he felt, to remember what he remembered.

For Whom It Was Written

This book was written for the seekers — for those who ask questions at night, for those who doubt yet still yearn, for those who want to make faith feel alive again.

It is for the student overwhelmed by deadlines, the parent searching for calm, the believer trying to make sense of hardship. It is for anyone who wants to speak to God not as an idea, but as a presence.

You do not need to know Arabic. You do not need to be a scholar. You only need to be honest — to bring your whole self to the page, and let these prayers meet you where you are.

How to Read This Book

There is no right or wrong order. You may start from the beginning and move through the journey, or open to any chapter that matches your heart's moment.

Each section begins with the Imam's voice — drawn from the Saḥīfa. Then comes reflection — how his duʿāʾ speaks to our lives today. Finally, every chapter closes with a short whisper or meditation — a moment to breathe, to feel, to respond.

You may read a few pages or stay with one prayer for days. Let it unfold slowly. The Imam's words are alive — they meet you differently each time.

A Living Conversation

Imam Zayn al-ʿĀbidīn (A.S) lived in the aftermath of unimaginable loss. Yet his response was not bitterness — it was beauty. He rebuilt the inner world of the community through the language of duʿāʾ — restoring dignity, faith, and hope through words.

His whispers teach that the most powerful speech is not public, but personal. That healing does not come from hiding your pain, but from surrendering it. That worship is not escape from the world, but engagement with it — with clearer sight and softer heart.

In his world, prayer was not about distance. It was about nearness — learning to see God in the everyday breath, the fleeting joy, the breaking moment.

The Journey Ahead

This book moves through twenty-four sections — each a doorway into a different human experience. Together they trace the path of the soul: from awareness to reflection, from struggle to patience, from love to service, from gratitude to reunion.

It begins with awakening — the heart's first remembrance — and ends with return — the soul's peaceful homecoming to the Divine. Between those two stations lies life itself: its fears, its beauty, its noise, its silence.

A Note to the Reader

As you turn these pages, let your reading become your prayer. Pause when a line stirs you. Underline what hurts and what heals. Whisper what feels true. This is not just a book — it is a mirror.

And somewhere, between your heartbeat and these words, you may feel what the Imam felt in his solitude — that faith, at its core, is simply the art of remembering who you have always belonged to.

"O God," he once prayed, "if I forget You, remind me of You.

And if I remember You, let my remembrance be my peace."

May these pages help you find that peace. May they light the lantern within you — until every breath becomes a whisper of praise.

AUTHOR'S NOTE — WHY THIS BOOK WAS WRITTEN

There are books that teach. And there are books that transform.

When I first opened As-Sahīfa al-Kāmilah al-Sajjādiyyah, I did not approach it as an expert or interpreter — only as a seeker, standing quietly at the edge of something sacred, trying to understand what it means to speak to God honestly.

The Sahīfa moved me in a way few texts ever had. It did not command; it invited. It did not preach; it whispered. Its voice was human — trembling, raw, luminous.

And I realised that this was not just a collection of supplications. It was an education of the heart.

Why Teens and Young Adults

When I began sharing these reflections, I saw how many young people felt disconnected from traditional forms of prayer — how the language sometimes felt distant, how faith seemed difficult to hold in the noise of modern life.

And yet, when they encountered the Imam's words — about fear, loneliness, ambition, regret, and love — they recognised themselves in them. They found their emotions named, their pain dignified, their hope reignited.

That is when this project became more than an adaptation. It became a conversation.

This book was written for those who wish to speak to God not in borrowed voices, but in their own.

A Bridge Between Eras

As-Sahīfa al-Kāmilah al-Sajjādiyyah was written in an age of oppression, yet its wisdom feels written for our time. The Imam lived through collapse and loss — and chose prayer as his way of rebuilding.

He reminded the world that faith can survive anything if it lives in the language of sincerity.

This work is a humble attempt to make that language accessible again — to carry the warmth, courage, and tenderness of his prayers into the rhythm of today's world.

Each chapter is born from his original supplications, retold as a journey of emotion, memory, and reflection. It moves slowly — like the Imam's own pauses between tears. It is meant to be felt, not rushed.

How to Use This Book

You don't have to read it all at once. Let it accompany you — quietly, like a friend.

Read one section when you wake, or one before you sleep. Carry a sentence with you through your day. Underline, annotate, whisper, reflect.

Each chapter is a mirror — it will show you something different every time.

And if one line stays with you, let that be your prayer for the day.

This book does not aim to replace the Imam's words — it aims to lead you back to them. To show how ancient supplications can still speak to modern restlessness, how the whisper of a saint can still calm a stormed heart.

A Personal Confession

While writing, there were nights I paused in silence. The depth of the Imam's words felt overwhelming — his humility, his grief, his trust.

Yet each time I hesitated, I remembered how his duʿās were born — not from comfort, but from courage.

That gave me strength to continue — to keep writing, to keep translating emotion into reflection, and to believe that faith, even in fragments, is still enough.

A Final Hope

My only prayer for this book is that it helps you fall in love again — with remembrance, with stillness, with your own soul.

If even one chapter becomes your mirror, if even one duʿāʾ feels like it was written for you, then this effort has been worth it.

"O God," the Imam prayed, "You are closer to me than my own breath.

When I forget You, You still remember me."

May you, dear reader, find in these pages not just inspiration — but intimacy.

May you learn to speak to God as you are, and hear, in return, the quiet assurance of His love.

CHAPTER ONE:
THE CALL TO AWARENESS

*Based on the Supplication of Praise and Gratitude to God
(Duʿā' 1 of the Sahifa al-Kamilah al-Sajjadiyya)*

1. The Quiet Hour Before Dawn

The city slept under a faint mist. Streetlights hummed softly, painting the pavement gold. Inside his small room, he sat cross-legged on the edge of the bed, a faint chill clinging to the early hour.

It was one of those mornings that arrives before you're ready — the kind that feels like time itself is waiting for you to notice it.

He didn't know why he had woken so early. His phone blinked on the bedside table, notifications glowing like restless stars. For once, he ignored them.

He rubbed his eyes, stretched, and sat in silence. The hum of the refrigerator. The distant call of a bird outside. The slow rhythm of his own breathing.

For the first time in what felt like months, he wasn't rushing toward anything.

And in that rare stillness, something unexpected stirred inside him — a small, persistent awareness that he was alive, that he was being held by something unseen.

It was a thought that should have been ordinary, yet it felt monumental.

He didn't say it aloud, but the words formed quietly in his mind: What if this stillness... is God calling me to notice?

2. The Voice of the Imam

From across centuries, a voice seemed to answer — calm, luminous, filled with reverence. It was not a command but an invitation.

"All praise is for God — the First, before any being existed, and the Last, after all things are gone. He is the Outward, whom no eyes can encompass, and the Inward, closer to the heart than its own beat.

He is the One whose blessings cannot be counted, whose praise cannot be described, whose mercy outlives every moment.

Praise be to God, who made Himself known to us before He made us know anyone else."

The words of Imam Zayn al-'Ābidīn (A.S) — spoken more than a thousand years ago — filled the silence like light pouring into a dark room.

The boy closed his eyes and imagined the Imam: a man of worship, living in the shadows of oppression, yet choosing to begin his prayers not with sorrow but with praise.

The Imam's world was filled with grief and hardship, yet his voice carried something otherworldly — gratitude that refused to fade. He was teaching that **awareness begins with wonder**, not fear.

3. Seeing What Was Always There

The boy stood and walked to the window. The mist had begun to lift, revealing rooftops soaked in faint gold. Every droplet on the glass caught the dawn.

He thought about how easily days blurred together — the endless routine of school, messages, noise, and tiredness. He had spent so long chasing what was next that he'd forgotten to notice what already was.

The Imam's words echoed softly in his heart: Praise be to God who made Himself known to us before He made us know anyone else.

What did it mean, he wondered, for God to make Himself known first? Maybe it meant that awareness isn't something we find at the end of a search; it's something we remember after forgetting. Maybe faith isn't about learning something new — it's about remembering something ancient that we always knew, deep down.

The Imam seemed to be whispering: You already know the truth, because it is written into your being.

4. Gratitude as Awareness

As the light brightened, he realised something profound — praise was not about flattery; it was about seeing clearly. The Imam's words were teaching him that gratitude is not a reaction to something good happening; it's a way of seeing the world as already drenched in blessing.

He remembered small mercies he'd ignored: His mother's voice calling him to breakfast. The quiet steadiness of his heart, beating without command. The strength of his body that carried him daily without complaint.

Each one, unnoticed until this moment, seemed like a verse from a silent scripture.

He understood now what the Imam meant when he said: "He whose praise the describers cannot describe, whose blessings the counters cannot count."

The more he thought about gratitude, the more endless it became. It was like trying to count sunlight or measure wind — impossible, yet beautiful to try.

5. The Awareness That Changes Everything

He sat back down, and this time he whispered — softly, sincerely: "Thank You."

Two words, fragile and human, but they felt like opening a window in the soul.

He realised that this is where faith truly begins — not in debates, or rituals, or grand gestures, but in the simple awareness that we are held, seen, sustained.

That was the Imam's secret. His entire Sahifa begins with that recognition: that everything we are, every breath we take, is an extension of mercy.

To be aware is to live in the company of God — even in silence, even in confusion.

6. The Meaning of the First Duʻa

The Imam's first supplication — the opening of the Sahifa al-Kamilah — is not a list of praises; it's a doorway into consciousness. Through each line, he's guiding us to remember where we came from, who sustains us, and what we owe back in return.

It's a dialogue, not a monologue. When the Imam says, "Praise be to God, the First and the Last," he's not describing God's timeline — he's describing the truth of our lives: that before our first breath and after our last, there is Presence. That all things come from Him and return to Him.

Awareness, then, is not a spiritual luxury — it's the ground beneath everything. It is the soil in which every other prayer takes root.

7. Living the Duʻa Today

When you walk to school. When you listen to rain tapping the window. When you look at your reflection and see a tired, imperfect person — that is the moment to whisper: "Praise be to God who made Himself known to me before I knew anyone else."

It means: Before I was anyone's friend, child, student, worker — I was already known by You. That's not a doctrine. That's intimacy.

Imam Sajjad is inviting us to live from that awareness every day — to turn daily life into a continuous remembrance. When you start your morning with gratitude, you walk differently.

You speak softer.

You see clearer.

That is what the Imam meant by "light in the heart."

8. The Whisper for Our Time

And if the Imam were here, speaking to our restless age, perhaps his words would sound like this:

"O my Lord, You were there before I opened my eyes. You are there when I forget, when I rush, when I stumble. Teach me to praise You not because You need my words, but because I need to remember.

Let me wake with awareness and sleep with gratitude. Let every breath remind me that I belong to mercy."

He might remind us that remembrance is freedom — freedom from fear, from comparison, from emptiness. To remember God is to return home.

9. Reflection for the Reader

Try this tonight:

Before you sleep, switch off the light and whisper three things you're grateful for — not big things, but the quiet ones. The way your lungs fill with air. The sound of someone laughing nearby. The feeling of safety when you close your eyes.

Then say softly: Praise be to God, the One whose mercy never leaves me.

This is how awareness begins — not with noise, but with noticing.

10. Closing Reflection

The Call to Awareness is not the prayer of a scholar; it's the cry of a soul rediscovering what it's made of. It tells us that before we can ask for forgiveness, or help, or strength — we must first see.

The Imam's first du'a is not just words to recite; it's a way to live awake. To live seeing mercy in everything. To live knowing that we are seen — always, endlessly, lovingly.

And when that awareness becomes part of your breathing, you'll understand why the Imam began where he did: with praise that opens the heart like dawn opens the sky.

Whispers of the Heart

CHAPTER TWO:
THE MIRROR OF THE SOUL

Based on Duʿāʾ 12: Confession and Seeking Forgiveness

1. The Weight of Quiet

The house was finally still. Even the hum of the refrigerator had quieted. Only the soft tapping of rain against the window broke the silence.

She sat at her desk, a notebook open, pen hovering above a blank page. Homework forgotten, phone silenced. Her reflection in the dark glass looked older than she felt — eyes tired, face uncertain.

It had been one of those weeks that left her restless. She had said things she didn't mean. She had ignored someone who needed her. She had prayed, but with distracted lips and an absent heart.

Now, with no noise left to hide behind, she felt the unease she had been avoiding — that faint ache of conscience that says: You can do better than this.

It wasn't guilt exactly; it was something deeper. A longing to be lighter.

2. The Whisper of the Imam

Into that silence, the voice of the Imam seemed to arrive — not scolding, but tender. It was the voice of someone who understood the exhaustion of carrying hidden things.

"O my God,

I wronged my own soul through heedlessness. My steps were unsteady, my eyes distracted, my heart clouded. I confess before You my failings and the slips that burden me.

You are the One who opens the door of mercy to those who knock. You call the heedless to remembrance. You accept the excuses of those who fall. You forgive the one who returns, even when he returns a thousand times."

Her breath caught. It was as though the Imam had taken her scattered feelings and given them words — not to shame her, but to set her free.

3. The Courage to Look Within

She picked up her pen and began to write — not an essay, not a prayer, but a truth. Every line began the same way: "I regret..."

"I regret being impatient."

"I regret pretending I didn't care."

"I regret not saying thank you."

The words came slowly at first, then faster, until the page was filled. As she wrote, she realised something she had never noticed before: admitting wrong didn't make her smaller — it made her real.

This was the mirror the Imam was speaking about — not a mirror that reflected the surface, but one that showed the soul. And when she finally saw herself clearly, she didn't see hopelessness. She saw a person capable of change.

That was the hidden mercy of confession: it turns guilt into movement, paralysis into prayer.

4. The Secret of the Imam's Duʿa

Imam Zayn al-ʿĀbidīn (A.S) doesn't speak like someone crushed by sin; he speaks like someone relieved by truth.

"My God, when I look upon Your mercy, I am filled with hope; but when I remember my deeds, I am overcome by shame.

Yet You, O Lord, are greater than my sins, and Your forgiveness broader than my misdeeds."

He's showing that repentance is not self-punishment — it's an act of trust. To confess is to say: I still believe You are kind. It's to believe that the same God who sees our mistakes also sees the goodness still struggling to breathe within us.

The Imam's language of confession isn't born from fear — it's born from love too deep to lie.

5. A Modern Mirror

She turned off her desk lamp. The rain outside had softened to a whisper. She thought of all the times she had apologised to people but never to herself — or to God. How many times she had said "I'm fine" when she wasn't.

She realised that self-honesty is one of the purest forms of prayer. It's standing before your Creator and saying, Here I am — unedited.

In a world obsessed with appearances, the Imam's voice is radical:

it calls us to unfiltered truth. To stand in the quiet and say: This is me — and still, I am loved.

6. The Turning Point

The Imam's duʿa continues:

"My God,

I have returned to You from my distance; I have come back after my turning away. Receive me with the welcome of one who has longed for his friend. Clothe me in the robe of Your pardon."

Those words changed the rhythm of her breathing. The idea that God could welcome her back — not coldly, not conditionally, but joyfully — felt almost impossible.

Yet that was the beauty of this prayer: The same lips that confess wrongdoing are invited to smile again. Because confession, in the Imam's way, is not about reminding yourself of how far you've fallen — it's about remembering how near you can still be.

7. The Mirror of Light

She closed her notebook and whispered softly: "O Lord, show me who I am — and show me who I could be."

In that moment, she felt as if her heart had turned into glass — transparent, fragile, but clean. That was the mirror of the soul: not polished perfection, but sincerity.

Imam Sajjad says in another prayer:

"O God, place Your light in my heart, Your insight in my sight, and the remembrance of You upon my tongue."

It was as if he was giving her the next step: after confession comes illumination.

The light doesn't erase the past; it shows how to walk differently now.

8. The Modern Whisper

"O God, I am tired of pretending to be fine. I am tired of carrying what I won't name.

You already know every mistake, every hesitation, every word I wish I could take back. Yet You still wait for me with open mercy.

Teach me to return — not out of fear, but because I miss being near You."

9. Reflection for the Reader

Try this:

Find a quiet place tonight. Bring a notebook.

Write one thing you wish you could do differently.

Then write one thing you're proud of having done right. Hold both truths in your hands — your weakness and your strength. That balance is where real repentance lives.

Then whisper:

"My Lord, if You have already forgiven me, teach me to forgive myself."

You'll find that the mirror of the soul reflects not only flaws, but possibilities.

10. Closing Reflection

The second step in the Imam's spiritual journey is not perfection — it's honesty. After awareness comes self-recognition. Only when the heart dares to look at itself can it begin to heal.

The Mirror of the Soul teaches that God's mercy is not a reward for the sinless, but a refuge for the sincere.

The Imam reminds us that to admit our weakness is not to fail faith — it's to prove it.

Because every time we turn toward the Divine and say, "I was wrong," He replies, "I have been waiting for you."

CHAPTER THREE:
THE WEIGHT OF WRONG

Based on Duʿāʾ 16: Seeking Pardon and Mercy

1 · The Walk Home in the Rain

The sky was the colour of ash. He walked home alone, hood pulled low, shoes soaking through. Rain slid down the back of his neck, cold enough to sting, yet he welcomed it. It matched the heaviness he felt inside.

He replayed the scene again and again—words he should never have said, a truth he twisted to save face, a friend's eyes filling with disappointment. Each replay made the silence louder.

By the time he reached the gate, guilt had turned physical: a stone behind the ribs, pressing. He didn't know if it was anger, shame, or sadness; only that something inside him wanted to kneel.

He thought of prayer but couldn't bring himself to speak. He felt too unworthy to start.

2 · The Voice of the Imam

Out of that numbness came a voice—not thunderous, but patient. It felt ancient, yet intimate, as though spoken directly into the storm.

"My God, my sins have weighed me down, my heedlessness has separated me from You.

I have wronged my own soul, yet I have nowhere to flee but toward Your mercy.

No one forgives sins except You; no one overlooks faults except You."

The rain seemed to pause on the windowsill. He could almost hear the Imam's breathing between lines—steady, compassionate. The words did not accuse; they invited.

He whispered, "That's me."

3 · The Anatomy of Guilt

He leaned against the wall, letting the dampness soak his sleeve. Guilt, he realised, was not punishment from God—it was a message from the soul saying, Come back.

He remembered the Imam's next line:

"When I remember Your mercy, I find hope; when I remember my deeds, I am overcome with shame.

Yet Your mercy is greater than my shame."

Those words shifted something. Maybe guilt was never meant to crush him; it was meant to open him. He had been confusing remorse with despair. The Imam was teaching the difference.

4 · The Weight Begins to Lift

He stepped inside, dripping water across the floor. Without thinking, he whispered:

"God, if You don't forgive me, who will?"

It wasn't recitation—it was instinct.

He felt no lightning, no sudden light, just the smallest loosening inside, as if a rope had been untied. He remembered another line:

"O Lord, even if You punish me, I will not despair of You; and if You forgive me, it will not surprise me— for You are accustomed to generosity."

He smiled through tears. How different this felt from fear. To speak honestly, to admit wrong, and still to be loved—this was freedom disguised as repentance.

5 · A Modern Mirror

He sat by his desk, phone buzzing with unread messages. How easily he could hide again—scroll, distract, forget. But something in him resisted. He opened the notes app instead and typed three sentences:

I hurt someone today.

I feel smaller for it.

But I want to be better.

That was it. No eloquence, no excuse. Yet it felt like the first real prayer he'd made in months.

He realised that confession isn't humiliation—it's clarity. And clarity, the Imam would say, is mercy's first spark.

6 · The Turning of the Heart

Later that night, he opened a small translation of the Sahifa and found more of the same supplication:

"O God, I come before You carrying the burden of what I have done. My tears are my plea, my silence my confession.

If You turn me away, who will receive me? But if You accept me, who can reject me?"

He let the book rest open on his knees. In those lines he recognised himself—not the version polished for others, but the real one, flawed yet still capable of grace.

That was when he understood: repentance is not about erasing the past; it's about transforming it into wisdom.

7 · The Gift of Forgiveness

He thought of the friend he had hurt. Tomorrow he would apologise. Not to fix his reputation, but to honour the forgiveness he had just received.

He remembered the Imam's final appeal:

"My Lord, make my repentance sincere; purify my heart from the stain of sin.

Replace my wrongdoing with goodness, so that my shame becomes gratitude."

It was redemption described as transformation: to take the ashes of guilt and turn them into the soil of growth.

8 · The Modern Whisper

"O Merciful One, teach me to face myself without fear.

Let my guilt not be a chain but a key.

When I remember what I've done, remind me also of what You can make of me.

Forgive me not only for the act, but for ever thinking I could live without Your light."

9 · Reflection for the Reader

This week:

Recall one mistake that still troubles you.

Write a letter to God beginning with *"I'm sorry..."* but end it with *"Thank You for still loving me."*

Then, if you can, apologise to the person or situation involved.

Repentance in Imam Sajjad's way is not only inward; it ripples outward, repairing what it touches.

10 · Closing Reflection

Awareness opened the eyes. Reflection opened the heart. Now, remorse opens the path home.

The Weight of Wrong is the chapter of turning—the sacred moment when pain becomes direction. Imam Zayn al-ʿĀbidīn (A.S) teaches that God's mercy is not earned by perfection but awakened by honesty.

Each tear shed in regret is a seed of renewal. And when those seeds bloom, they whisper the same truth:

You are never too far gone to begin again.

Whispers of the Heart

CHAPTER FOUR:
THE QUIET BATTLE

Based on Duʿāʾ 7: In Hardship and Difficulty, Duʿāʾ 14: Seeking Refuge, and the Whispered Prayer of the Fearful

1 · The Long Night

The clock glowed 2:13 a.m. The world outside her window was quiet — too quiet — but her mind refused to rest.

Every thought spun into another: exams, friendships, the future, the silence of unanswered prayers. She rolled over again, eyes stinging, heart racing. Sleep had become a stranger.

In that darkness, she whispered the words she was afraid to say out loud:

"I don't know how much longer I can keep this up."

The ceiling above her felt heavy. Even prayer felt far away — a language she used to know but somehow forgot.

It wasn't rebellion that kept her from praying — it was exhaustion. She didn't want to talk to God with a fake calm voice. She wanted to cry without explanation.

2 · The Voice of the Imam

Then, in that thick silence, a gentle voice seemed to rise — ancient yet intimate, steady as breath itself.

"O God, my distress has overwhelmed me. My patience has weakened, my strength has diminished.

I have no refuge except in You. No one can ease what You have made difficult, and no one can make difficult what You have made easy.

In Your hands lie the keys of relief."

The words didn't promise the end of pain. They promised presence in the middle of it.

She pulled her blanket closer and breathed in slowly. The Imam's tone was not desperate — it was deliberate. It sounded like a man who had learned that surrender is stronger than resistance.

3 · Understanding Hardship

She thought of how quickly life could turn — how one moment you feel steady, and the next, everything tilts.

But maybe, she realised, hardship isn't always punishment. Maybe it's God's way of uncovering where we've been relying too much on ourselves.

The Imam's next line came to her memory:

"My Lord, in every trial, You are my hope. In every fear, You are my refuge.

You are the shelter for the frightened, the helper of the oppressed, the comforter of the sorrowful."

It was strange comfort — not the kind that erased pain, but the kind that made pain bearable.

Patience, she thought, isn't pretending you're okay. It's whispering I still trust You even when everything hurts.

4 · The Hidden Strength of Surrender

She remembered something her grandmother once told her:

"Patience isn't sitting still; it's walking forward while your heart trembles."

The Imam's words seemed to echo that wisdom:

"O God, if You afflict me, it is with justice; and if You show mercy, it is from Your generosity.

My refuge is in Your pardon, my hope in Your kindness."

She felt the tension in her shoulders begin to soften. The fear hadn't disappeared, but it had lost its dominance.

There was something powerful in letting go of control — in admitting, I can't fix this, but You can hold me through it.

That surrender didn't feel weak; it felt sacred.

5 · The Modern Mirror

Later, she went downstairs and poured a glass of water. The night air was cool, almost metallic. She sat by the window and watched raindrops tracing the glass.

For the first time, she didn't feel like escaping her thoughts. She just let them drift, the way raindrops slide until gravity takes them home.

It occurred to her that the Imam's prayers were not for saints — they were for people like her, restless at 2 a.m., fighting quiet battles no one else could see.

She whispered, "O God, I'm tired of pretending to be strong."

The whisper turned into a kind of peace — fragile, but real.

6 · The Whisper of Refuge

Another line surfaced from the Whispered Prayer of the Fearful:

"My Lord, if You are with me, what can harm me? And if You abandon me, what can help me?

I seek refuge in You from my own weakness, and from every fear that steals my calm."

Those words felt like a blanket — not to hide beneath, but to rest under. She realised that fear isn't a failure of faith; it's an invitation to deeper trust.

Even the Prophet and his family had fears — but they learned to hold those fears inside the vastness of God's mercy.

Imam Sajjad was teaching her the same lesson across a thousand years: That the heart is strongest when it bows.

7 · The Modern Whisper

"O my Sustainer, calm the storms within me.

When my patience runs dry, let my tears become prayers.

When my strength falters, remind me that You never sleep.

Let me find rest not in control, but in surrender.

For even when I am silent, You are not absent."

8 · Reflection for the Reader

If tonight feels heavy, try this:

Sit somewhere quiet.

Place your hand over your heart and breathe deeply.

Whisper: *"In this moment, I am held."*

Then think of three things that make you anxious. After each one, say aloud: "But God knows."

You'll notice the tension doesn't vanish — it shifts. It becomes softer, smaller, more bearable.

That's the beginning of patience.

9 · Closing Reflection

The Quiet Battle never truly ends; it simply changes shape. There will always be moments of fear, fatigue, and waiting.

But Imam Zayn al-ʿĀbidīn (A.S) teaches that faith is not about avoiding storms — it's about finding the One who walks with you through them.

Patience, in his language, is love stretched across time. It is believing that every hardship is a message saying:

"I am still here — keep walking."

So when the next long night comes, and you find yourself awake at 2:13 a.m., remember: the battle is not yours to win; it is yours to witness. And the One who watches with you never sleeps.

Whispers of the Heart

CHAPTER FIVE:
THE GIFT OF GRATITUDE

Based on Duʿāʾ 35: Morning and Evening, and theWhispered Prayer of the Thankful

1 · The Morning Light

The world was still half-asleep when he opened the window. The air smelled faintly of dew and cut grass. Somewhere, a bird sang — one clear note, then another.

He leaned against the sill, eyes tired, body slow to wake. It had been another long week — endless messages, noise, deadlines, moments that felt hollow. But today, before touching his phone, he simply stood there and breathed.

The light was soft and pale, spilling gently across the sky like a quiet promise.

For once, he didn't rush the moment. He let the silence breathe with him.

That was when it came — the unexpected feeling that this ordinary morning was enough. He didn't need anything else.

2 · The Whisper of the Imam

It was as though the dawn itself began to speak — the voice of Imam Zayn al-ʿĀbidīn (A.S) carried on the early breeze:

"Praise belongs to God who has made the morning light rise for us, and clothed us with its brightness.

Praise belongs to God who has awakened us from sleep, and set before us the share of our sustenance.

Praise belongs to God who lets us witness day after night, and night after day — each a reminder of His mercy."

The Imam's words turned the simple act of waking into worship. They taught that every sunrise is a renewal of grace — an unseen hand resetting the soul for another chance to try again.

He whispered the words softly:

"Praise belongs to God who has awakened me."

And it felt as though his heart had opened a window of its own.

3 · Gratitude as Vision

He thought about how easy it was to live blind — to wake, eat, walk, scroll, sleep — and call that living. How many mornings had he missed because he was already somewhere else in his head?

But the Imam's voice made him see differently:

Gratitude was not just something you said — it was a way of seeing.

To say "al-ḥamdulillāh" was to acknowledge that nothing was ordinary — not even breath.

"Praise belongs to God," the Imam said, "for every mercy that is renewed with each breath."

It was stunning to think that gratitude was not about getting more — it was about noticing what had already been overflowing.

4 · The Modern Mirror

He remembered being a child, fascinated by everything: the way sunlight caught the dust, how raindrops made tiny worlds on the window. Back then, wonder was effortless.

Now, older, he'd traded that wonder for efficiency. Everything was measured by speed, productivity, achievement. Even gratitude had become something to check off a list.

But this morning, he realised — the Imam was calling him back to that childlike wonder, to see again through eyes washed in awe.

Maybe that's what the Whispered Prayer of the Thankful meant when it said:

"O God, how can I thank You, when my very act of thanking is a gift from You?

For every time I say 'thank You,' You give me more to thank You for."

It was gratitude as a spiral — each moment leading to another. An infinite loop of mercy and awareness.

5 · The Rhythm of Morning and Evening

He sat down with his cup of tea and opened the window wider. The city was waking now — cars starting, voices rising. But instead of feeling drowned by it, he felt strangely at peace.

He remembered the Imam's duʿa again, describing how the believer greets each day and night:

"O my God, this is a new day You have brought into being, and a fresh moment You have unfolded.

As long as the morning remains, let me fill it with gratitude.

And when night covers the earth again, let my last words be praise."

He realised the rhythm of the Sahifa was the rhythm of life itself — morning and evening, gain and loss, light and shadow — and gratitude was the thread that held it all together.

To live like the Imam was to praise through every phase.

6 · Finding Joy in the Small Things

He looked around: the steam curling from his mug, the ticking of the kitchen clock, the smell of toast from downstairs. All of it seemed touched by a quiet sacredness.

He remembered another line from the Imam:

"Praise belongs to God, who feeds us when we are hungry, gives us rest when we are weary, and shelters us in our homes."

Nothing dramatic, nothing grand — just daily mercies that most people never notice. And yet, this was where real joy lived: in the small, steady kindness of being cared for.

7 · The Modern Whisper

"O God, let me not overlook Your everyday mercies.

Teach me to thank You for the air I breathe, the water that runs clear, the safety of my home, and the warmth of being loved.

Do not let me wait for big miracles when You've hidden a thousand small ones in plain sight."

8 · Reflection for the Reader

Tonight or tomorrow morning:

Before looking at your phone, whisper: "Praise belongs to God who has awakened me."

Look around your room and list five blessings you can see right now — not abstract ones, but visible mercies.

Take a slow breath between each and say al-ḥamdulillāh aloud.

You'll find that gratitude doesn't change your circumstances — it changes your sight. And when you see differently, even routine feels radiant.

9 · Closing Reflection

Gratitude, in Imam Sajjad's world, is not an occasional response — it's the heartbeat of faith. It is how you breathe when you realise that life itself is prayer.

He teaches that to thank God is to stay awake to His presence — to move through the world in constant awareness that nothing you have is random, and that every ordinary moment is laced with extraordinary mercy.

The Gift of Gratitude is the realisation that joy doesn't arrive with success, or wealth, or recognition.

It lives quietly in the familiar —in breath, in bread, in sunrise.

And when you finally see that, you understand what the Imam meant:

To live gratefully is to live near God.

Whispers of the Heart

CHAPTER SIX:
THE BONDS THAT RAISED ME

Based on Duʿāʾ 24, 25, and 26:
For Parents, Children, and Neighbours

1 · The Call Home

It was one of those ordinary afternoons that pass unnoticed — grey clouds, coffee gone cold, inbox full. Her phone vibrated across the desk.

A text from her mother:

Did you eat?

No punctuation, no emojis. Just three words.

She sighed and smiled, half-amused, half-annoyed. She was twenty-three now, living alone in a new city, yet her mother still texted her every day. Sometimes it felt suffocating; other times, it was the only message that broke the silence.

She didn't reply right away. But as the evening fell and she walked home under a light drizzle, those words returned again — Did you eat?

She realised it was more than a question. It was a prayer disguised as habit.

2 · The Voice of the Imam

From the stillness of the walk, another voice seemed to rise — older, deeper, filled with compassion.

"O God, bless my parents as they raised me when I was small. Reward them for the care they gave me, for the sleepless nights they spent worrying over me, for every pain they concealed so that I could smile.

Let me remember their kindness in my strength, and honour them in their weakness.

Forgive them as they forgave me when I knew no better."

It was Imam Zayn al-'Ābidīn's (A.S) Supplication for His Parents. It didn't sound like duty — it sounded like love shaped into prayer.

He wasn't asking only for their long life or forgiveness; he was asking for the grace to see them as God sees them.

She thought of her own parents — all the things she never thanked them for because she assumed they didn't need thanks. Suddenly, even their ordinary texts felt sacred.

3 · Memory and Mercy

That night, she sat on her bed and scrolled through old photos: birthdays, blurry school plays, road trips, hospital visits, the little notes her mother used to leave in her lunchbox. She could almost hear her father's laughter in the background, the rhythm of safety that built her childhood.

She realised she had outgrown their house but not their prayers. Somewhere, perhaps at that very moment, her parents were still whispering her name into the night, asking God to keep her safe.

"O Lord," the Imam had said,

"join them to me in kindness,

and join me to them in mercy."

He understood what few remember — that family bonds are not just bloodlines, but channels of divine mercy.

4 · The Voice of the Imam — For Children

Then the Imam's voice turned from child to parent:

"O God, protect my children from harm, adorn them with faith and good character, and let me see in them the beauty of obedience to You.

Make me gentle toward them as You have been gentle toward me.

Help me to guide them not with harshness, but with compassion that teaches."

She paused, reading those lines in a small translation she kept by her bedside. It struck her that the Imam prayed not for control, but for care. Not that his children would succeed by worldly measures, but that they would live honourably, kindly, faithfully.

She imagined her parents doing the same all these years — not just wanting her to thrive, but to remain good. That was love in its purest form: concern that reached beyond comfort.

5 · The Circle of Care

Love, she realised, always travels in circles. The hands that once fed her would one day tremble; the voices that once guided her would one day grow quiet. And when that time came, her role would change — from being cared for to becoming the carer.

That's what the Imam meant when he prayed:

"O Lord, help me to serve them in their old age with the same tenderness they showed me as a child.

Do not let me raise my voice above theirs, nor forget their prayers when they are gone."

It wasn't repayment; it was continuation. The mercy we receive is the mercy we are meant to pass on.

6 · The Modern Mirror

A few days later, she visited home for the weekend. The kitchen smelled like cardamom and home. Her mother scolded her for not wearing enough layers, then handed her a plate of food before she could answer.

She laughed, suddenly overwhelmed by gratitude. Every tiny action — folding laundry, cutting fruit, worrying — was worship in disguise.

She remembered the Imam's words again:

"Bless the hearts that show love without expecting thanks. Bless the hands that give without measure. Bless the ones whose patience teaches us the meaning of Yours."

That night, she finally replied to that old message. Yes, Mama. I ate. And I love you.

7 · The Whisper for Family

"O God,

let me love them as You love me — patiently, endlessly, without keeping count.

Let my heart soften when they repeat the same advice. Let my gratitude grow deeper with every wrinkle I see.

When I become a parent, remind me of what they endured. And when they are gone, let my prayers reach them like the echoes of all the love they gave me."

8 · Reflection for the Reader

Try this tonight:

If your parents are alive, call them — not to talk about plans or errands, but just to say thank you.

If they are far away, send a message of love.

If they have returned to God, whisper this line from the Imam: "O God, forgive my parents, as they forgave me when I erred."

Then think about one way you can carry their mercy forward — by helping a sibling, comforting a friend, or simply being kind to someone else's child.

Because family, in the Imam's world, extends beyond the walls of a home.

9 · Closing Reflection

The Bonds That Raised Me is not only about parents or children — it is about the architecture of mercy that builds human life.

Imam Zayn al-ʿĀbidīn (A.S) teaches that every relationship — parent to child, neighbour to neighbour, friend to friend — is a reflection of divine compassion.

When you care for those who cared for you, when you forgive the ones who hurt you, when you pray for others before yourself — you are walking the same path of love that the Imam walked.

And one day, when your own child, friend, or student asks you, "Why do you love me this much?"

you can answer, *"Because Someone loved me first."*

CHAPTER SEVEN:
CIRCLES OF TRUST

Based on Duʿāʾ 27 and 38:
For Friends and For Neighbours

1 · The Empty Bench

The park was nearly empty. Autumn leaves drifted across the path, crisp and weightless, whispering secrets to the wind.

He sat down on the old wooden bench — the one he and his best friend used to claim every Saturday after football, laughing over shared jokes that only made sense to them.

But that was months ago, before the argument. Before pride had built its quiet wall between them.

Now the space beside him felt colder than the air. He stared at the spot where his friend used to sit — the easy grin, the shoulder bumps, the plans that once felt permanent.

And all he could think was how fragile trust really is.

2 · The Voice of the Imam — For Friends

In that silence, another voice began to echo — calm, steady, and ancient. It felt as though Imam Zayn al-ʿĀbidīn (A.S) himself were sitting beside him on that empty bench.

"O God, bless my friends with Your mercy. Strengthen the bonds between our hearts.

Teach us loyalty in absence, sincerity in speech, and gentleness in our faults toward one another.

Let not the envy of the envious divide us, nor the whispers of pride make us forget our love."

The Imam's prayer wasn't a plea for perfect companions. It was a call to be the kind of friend who forgives, who sees through hurt, who stays even when it would be easier to walk away.

He realised that what he missed most wasn't just the friendship — it was the version of himself that friendship had brought out: lighter, kinder, more open.

3 · The Nature of True Companionship

Friendship, in the Imam's world, was not just comfort — it was character. It revealed who you were when no one was watching.

"A true friend," the Imam teaches through his words and example, "is one whose presence reminds you of God, and whose absence makes you pray for them."

He remembered all the times his friend had been there — listening without judgement, pushing him to try again, sitting silently during heartbreaks when words weren't needed.

Now, looking back, he understood: loyalty wasn't about always agreeing —it was about always caring.

4 · The Modern Mirror

He scrolled through old messages on his phone. There it was — the last conversation, sharp words typed too quickly, pride disguised as honesty.

He hadn't been wrong, maybe. But he hadn't been gentle either. And the silence that followed felt heavier than any victory.

He thought of the Imam's prayer again:

"O Lord,

do not let my love for them turn into harm, nor my anger erase years of kindness."

He sighed, the kind of sigh that carries more than air — the weight of regret, of realising that being right is often less important than being kind.

The screen glowed back at him, waiting.

He began to type:

"Hey, I miss our talks. I'm sorry for how I reacted that day."

He didn't overthink it. He just sent it. And in that small act, something inside him softened — the bench didn't feel so empty anymore.

5 · The Voice of the Imam — For the Community

Later that evening, as the streetlights flickered on, he walked home through his neighbourhood. He saw the same faces he often passed — the old man sweeping his front porch, the kids cycling past, the woman from next door carrying groceries. He'd never really looked at them — not seen them.

But then another of the Imam's supplications came to mind:

"O God, bless my neighbours and my people.

Make us a source of comfort, not conflict; protect us from envy and harm.

Let our streets be filled with peace, our hearts with mercy for one another."

It struck him how Imam Sajjad didn't separate spirituality from society. For him, loving God meant loving people. To care for your community was itself a form of prayer.

He smiled at the old man sweeping leaves and helped him gather the pile. "Thank you," the man said, surprised. He just nodded — "It's nothing." But deep down, it felt like something sacred.

6 · The Modern Whisper

"O God,

make me the kind of friend who heals, not hurts.

Let my words be bridges, not walls.

When I am loved, keep me humble. When I am hurt, keep me gentle.

Let me walk beside others the way You walk beside me — quietly, faithfully, without end."

7 · Reflection for the Reader

This week, think of one friendship that has faded or cracked. Don't wait for a grand apology. Send a small message — something simple like "I hope you're doing okay."

You'll be surprised how much light that small act can let back in.

Then, look around your community. Smile at someone you usually walk past. Offer help where no one expects it. That's how you rebuild the circles of trust that keep the world humane.

8 · Closing Reflection

The Circles of Trust begin small — two people, a word of kindness, a moment of forgiveness — but they ripple outward. They become families, communities, nations.

Imam Zayn al-ʿĀbidīn's (A.S) duʿas teach that friendship is not an accident of affection; it is a conscious choice to nurture compassion in a world that often forgets how to love gently.

He teaches that every hand you hold, every apology you make, every time you choose mercy over pride — you are building the kind of world his prayers envisioned.

And perhaps one day, when someone sits on that same park bench, they'll remember your laughter too, and whisper a prayer for you — the kind that keeps friendship alive long after words fade.

Whispers of the Heart

CHAPTER EIGHT:
LESSONS AND LEARNING

Based on Duʿāʾ 23 and the Treatise on Rights

1 · The Library Light

The clock struck midnight in the old university library. Rows of books stood like silent witnesses, and the fluorescent light hummed softly overhead.

He sat hunched over a pile of notes, eyes red, mind fogged with formulas and deadlines. The glow of his laptop screen reflected in the untouched cup of coffee beside him. He was exhausted — not from studying, but from chasing.

He wanted good grades, a good job, a good future. But somewhere in the rush, he had lost the joy of learning itself.

He rubbed his temples and whispered, almost to himself,

"Why do I feel so full of facts, yet so empty of meaning?"

The silence answered him with stillness — until, faintly, another voice began to rise.

2 · The Voice of the Imam — The Prayer for Knowledge

It wasn't the voice of a lecturer or a motivational quote; it was older, steadier — the tone of someone who had studied the soul before books ever existed.

"O God, adorn me with knowledge, and guard me from ignorance.

Let me not seek learning for pride or competition, but for the light it brings to the heart.

Teach me that the best of knowledge is that which draws me nearer to You."

The words of Imam Zayn al-ʿĀbidīn (A.S) settled over him like dawn breaking over a restless sea.

He'd been treating study as a race — the Imam was reminding him it was a pilgrimage.

3 · The Burden of Knowing

He leaned back in his chair, staring at the ceiling, thinking about how strange it was that knowledge, meant to illuminate, sometimes left people darker.

He'd seen classmates boast about grades, argue over who was smarter, turn study into rivalry.

He wasn't innocent of it himself. He remembered the rush of being praised, the anxiety of losing that praise — how quickly learning had become performance.

And yet, in the Imam's duʿāʾ, there was another kind of student: one who studied not to excel, but to elevate.

"O Lord, let me act upon what I know, and let my knowledge benefit others."

The line echoed through him like a slow bell. It was as if the Imam was teaching that information becomes wisdom only when it changes how you treat people.

4 · The Modern Mirror

He thought of his favourite teacher — a quiet man with a crooked smile who once told him, "You don't truly know something until you can explain it with kindness."

At the time, he didn't understand. Now he did.

Learning wasn't meant to make him important; it was meant to make him useful.

He remembered how Imam Sajjad wrote in his Treatise on Rights:

"Know that your teacher has the right of a parent.

He has delivered you from the darkness of ignorance to the light of knowledge.

So honour him as you would your father."

He realised he had spent years thanking his teachers with grades but rarely with gratitude. The Imam was reminding him that real honour isn't shown in results — it's shown in reverence.

5 · The Humility of Understanding

He looked down at his open notebook — pages filled with underlined facts, arrows, and notes. But the most important line he wrote that night was in the margin:

"Knowledge without humility blinds the heart."

He thought again of the Imam's words:

"O God, do not raise me in knowledge while lowering me in humility.

Let me never forget that all learning is borrowed light."

He felt the tension ease — the weight of expectation, the endless comparison. For the first time in weeks, he felt free.

The purpose of knowledge wasn't to prove oneself — it was to know the One who gave all knowing.

6 · The Whisper of the Imam

He closed his books, pressed his palms together, and recited softly into the quiet air:

"O Lord, teach me what will benefit me, and make me benefit others by what You teach.

Keep my mind clear and my intentions pure. Let every lesson I learn become a bridge — from ignorance to service, from pride to peace."

It wasn't a study plan. It was a surrender.

7 · The Modern Whisper

"O God,

let my curiosity never fade, but keep it kind.

Let me read not only books, but hearts.

Let me listen more than I speak.

Let my knowledge not make me proud, but patient.

For the truest wisdom is to remain teachable."

8 · Reflection for the Reader

Try this:

Write down one thing you've learned this month that made you gentler, not smarter.

Then, think of one person who taught you something meaningful — a teacher, friend, parent, even a stranger.

Say a quiet prayer for them tonight:

"O God, bless the ones who opened my mind, and forgive me when I forgot to thank them."

And if you are a teacher — in any form — whisper this: "O God, let my words reach hearts, not just ears."

9 · Closing Reflection

Knowledge, in Imam Sajjad's world, is not a ladder to status — it's a lamp for service. It shines brightest when shared.

He teaches that every learner must become a giver, and every act of learning should make the soul softer, the mind humbler, and the world kinder.

The Lessons and Learning of the Imam remind us that intellect itself is a form of worship. When the mind bows in humility, it becomes a place of light.

And in that light, even the smallest act — reading, thinking, asking — becomes a way of remembering the One who taught humanity the gift of knowing.

CHAPTER NINE:
EARNING AND ENOUGHNESS

Based on Duʿāʾ 18 and 19:
Seeking Provision and Against Greed

1 · The Late Paycheck

It was one of those months where everything came due at once — rent, electricity, the phone bill, even the annual insurance renewal.

He sat at his small kitchen table, calculator open, receipts spread like fallen leaves. The kettle hissed in the background. His stomach tightened with that familiar anxiety — the quiet panic of not knowing if you'll have enough.

He worked hard, he told himself. He wasn't lazy. But every time he thought he was ahead, life found a way to remind him he wasn't.

He whispered under his breath, "Why does it always feel like this?"

There was no anger in his voice — just fatigue.

He didn't want wealth; he just wanted ease.

2 · The Voice of the Imam — Seeking Provision

The night outside was still. He leaned back in his chair, closed his eyes, and let the Imam's words rise from memory like a balm:

"O God, bless my provision.

Do not test me through scarcity that drives me to despair, nor through abundance that tempts me to arrogance.

Make me content with what You have allotted to me, and keep me safe from craving what is beyond my share."

He opened his eyes slowly. The tone wasn't one of desperation; it was balance — a middle way between striving and surrender.

The Imam didn't ask for riches. He asked for contentment.

That line lingered like a whisper in the quiet: "Make me content with what You have allotted to me."

3 · The Weight of Wanting

He looked at the stack of unpaid bills again. They seemed smaller somehow. Still real, still demanding — but less threatening.

He realised something: his stress wasn't only about money. It was about control.

He wanted certainty, predictability — a guarantee that tomorrow would be safe. But the Imam was teaching him something radical: that provision isn't only what you earn — it's what you trust.

"O Lord, You are the One who feeds all creation.

None goes hungry except by their forgetfulness of You."

He thought about how much energy he'd spent chasing what he already had in some measure — shelter, warmth, food, breath.

He'd been so busy worrying about "what if" that he'd stopped noticing "what is."

4 · The Modern Mirror

He remembered a few years back — a time when he had a higher-paying job, nicer clothes, and endless overtime. He had more money, but less peace. Weekends blurred into workdays, and every success felt smaller than the last.

Then he remembered another period — after he'd been laid off, when he lived on savings and simplicity. Oddly enough, those days felt lighter. He'd had less, but he'd laughed more, slept better, prayed deeper.

The difference wasn't his bank balance. It was his balance within.

The Imam's prayer echoed again in his thoughts:

"Do not let greed blind me to gratitude, nor desire distract me from remembrance."

It was astonishing — how the same few words could untangle years of worry.

5 · The Voice of the Imam — Against Greed

He turned a page in the Sahifa al-Kamilah and found the next supplication — a warning disguised as mercy:

"O God, protect me from the craving of greed, and from stretching my hand toward that which is not mine.

Let me not measure my worth by what I own, but by the peace that dwells in my heart."

He read it twice.

That's what this was about — not rejection of work or ambition, but purification of intention.

To work for sustenance was a duty. To worship wealth was a chain.

The Imam wasn't preaching poverty; he was teaching proportion — that what matters most is not how much you gather, but how much gratitude you carry.

6 · The Whisper of the Imam

He closed the book and whispered softly into the dim room:

"O God, give me hands that work, and a heart that rests.

Let my earnings be clean, my spending moderate, and my sleep peaceful.

If You give me wealth, make me generous.

If You test me with little, make me patient."

He smiled faintly — the kind of smile that rises not from happiness, but from understanding.

The numbers on the table hadn't changed. But the heaviness inside him had lifted.

7 · The Modern Whisper

"O Sustainer of hearts, calm the restlessness that makes me forget Your promise.

Teach me to work with trust, to plan without fear, and to give without counting.

Let my income be clean, my wants few, and my gratitude vast. Let me live not chasing more, but celebrating enough."

8 · Reflection for the Reader

This week:

Make a list of what you already have — the things you prayed for once and now take for granted.

Read that list slowly, aloud if you can.

Whisper: *"This is my rizq, and I am grateful."*

If you're struggling with finances, pray with the Imam's balance: ask for sufficiency, not excess; for ease, not escape.

And if you find yourself blessed with abundance, remember: the test of wealth is generosity.

9 · Closing Reflection

In a world that measures worth by numbers, Imam Zayn al-'Ābidīn's (A.S) voice is a reminder from eternity: that what sustains you is not your salary, but your Source.

Earning, when done with honesty, is worship. Spending, when done with gratitude, is wisdom. And trusting, when done with patience, is peace.

The Earning and Enoughness of the Imam isn't a call to abandon ambition — it's an invitation to align it.

Because when you finally learn to say, *"What I have is enough,"* you discover that you were rich all along.

Whispers of the Heart

CHAPTER TEN:
BODY AND BREATH

*Based on Duʿāʾ 15 and 6:
In Illness and For the Sick*

1 · The Fever Night

The room was dim, the light from the streetlamps slicing thinly through the blinds. She lay curled beneath a blanket, her breath shallow, skin hot, head heavy with fever. The world outside moved on — traffic, laughter, life — but here, everything slowed.

Every sound felt amplified: the ticking clock, the kettle boiling, her own heartbeat echoing in her ears. She had always been the strong one — the one who managed, organised, fixed. But now even lifting a glass of water felt like lifting a mountain.

In the stillness of that night, she realised how fragile the body really was. How quickly certainty could become silence.

Her thoughts wandered, not to doctors or medicine, but to prayer — the kind whispered through weakness.

2 · The Voice of the Imam — In Illness

A voice rose gently in the quiet — calm, humble, intimate:

"O God, here I am, lying before You, weak, weary, and helpless.

My strength has left me, my tongue falters in remembrance, yet my heart still turns toward You.

If this illness is a test, then let my patience be my answer."

It was Imam Zayn al-ʿĀbidīn's (A.S) Duʿāʾ in Illness. His words did not ask why he was suffering. They asked how he could find meaning within it.

He called weakness not a curse, but a teacher — a mirror showing the limits of human control, and the vastness of divine mercy.

She whispered the line to herself:

"If this illness is a test, let my patience be my answer."

Something softened in her chest — not relief, not healing, but acceptance.

3 · The Meaning of Fragility

In health, she had felt unstoppable. Her calendar was full, her pace relentless. She never noticed her breath — until it grew shallow. She never thanked her body — until it trembled.

Now, in this stillness, every breath felt sacred. She remembered what the Imam had said:

"My God, You have clothed me in the robe of well-being so many times that I forgot it was Yours to give.

Forgive me for the days I woke strong and did not praise You."

She felt the sting of those words. How many mornings had she risen without gratitude, as if health were a right and not a gift?

Perhaps this fever, she thought, was not punishment. Perhaps it was remembrance.

4 · The Modern Mirror

The next morning, the fever broke. She sat by the window, pale but peaceful. The tea steamed gently in her hands; her body still weak, but her mind unusually clear.

She thought about all the times she had rushed through life — the meals eaten standing, the prayers shortened by hurry, the calls ignored because she was "too busy."

Now, in her slowed state, she saw the blessing in slowness.

Illness had stripped away everything unnecessary, and left behind only what mattered: stillness, breath, presence.

"O Lord," the Imam had prayed, "heal me with the healing of Your mercy, and let my sickness purify me from heedlessness."

She understood that line now. Healing wasn't just physical recovery. It was spiritual awakening — to live again with awareness.

5 · The Voice of the Imam — For the Sick

Later that week, as her strength returned, she found herself praying not only for herself, but for others — those in hospitals, in pain, unseen.

She opened her book again and read:

"O God, heal the sick among the people of Your mercy. Strengthen the weak, lighten the burden of those who suffer.

Make illness a door through which they draw nearer to You, not a wall that shuts them out."

She paused. Even in his own weakness, the Imam prayed for others. That was the truest sign of spiritual health: compassion that survives even in pain.

6 · The Whisper of the Imam

That night, before sleep, she whispered softly:

"O Healer of hearts, You know the weakness I hide.

When my body falters, hold my soul steady.

Let this pain cleanse, not consume.

Teach me that even when I cannot move, I can still turn toward You."

The room was silent. But something deep within her stirred — a peace she hadn't known in years.

7 · The Modern Whisper

"O God, if I must endure this, let me find You in it.

When I am too weak to pray, let my breath become my prayer.

When I am afraid, remind me that You are closer than the ache itself.

Heal me where medicine cannot reach — in the places that only faith can touch."

8 · Reflection for the Reader

If you are unwell — in body, mind, or heart — know that the Imam's voice reaches you here, too. He does not promise quick cures; he offers companionship through the pain.

Try this:

When you feel pain or fatigue, whisper: "This moment belongs to God."

Breathe slowly. With each breath, imagine gratitude entering, worry leaving.

If you know someone ill, send them a prayer from the Imam: "O God, heal them with Your mercy, and ease their hardship with Your nearness."

Sometimes the smallest whisper carries the deepest healing.

9 · Closing Reflection

Imam Zayn al-ʿĀbidīn (A.S) lived a life marked by suffering — the wounds of Karbala, the weight of survival, the frailty of his body. Yet from that frailty, he gave the world the most eloquent words of strength.

In his prayers, illness becomes illumination, and weakness becomes worship.

The Body and Breath of the Imam teaches that every heartbeat is a reminder — that we are not self-sustaining, that every act of breathing is mercy renewed.

And when sickness comes, it is not to break us, but to remind us whose hands have held us all along.

Healing, after all, is not the absence of pain — but the presence of God within it.

Whispers of the Heart

CHAPTER ELEVEN:
THE VOICE OF SERVICE

Based on Duʿāʾ 23, 27, and 47:
Praying for Others, For Friends, and For Nearness to God

1 · The Train Platform

It was one of those cold mornings when the city moved like a single restless creature — everyone rushing, faces down, minds already ahead of their bodies.

He stood on the crowded train platform, clutching his coffee, watching people stream past him: a mother juggling her child's hand and her phone, an elderly man balancing on a cane, a teenager staring at his reflection in the window.

He didn't know any of them. Yet, for a moment, he felt their weariness as his own.

He wondered — when was the last time he had truly prayed for someone else? Not the usual "hope you're well" kind of prayer, but a sincere, silent reaching of the heart.

It had been too long.

2 · The Voice of the Imam — Prayer for Others

In that crowded, noisy station, a calmer voice began to echo in his thoughts — not loud, but luminous, like dawn after a long night.

"O God, bless those who serve Your creation.

Strengthen their hearts when others forget them. Reward their patience, and keep their intentions pure.

Let the ones who carry others' burdens not collapse beneath their own."

He remembered that Imam Zayn al-ʿĀbidīn (A.S), even while living through grief and oppression, found the strength to pray for others — soldiers, workers, travellers, believers — every soul engaged in some unseen service.

The Imam's compassion wasn't limited by proximity; it expanded to humanity itself.

In that moment, surrounded by strangers, he felt the truth of those words: to pray for another is to widen the walls of one's heart.

3 · The Meaning of Service

He boarded the train, took a seat by the window, and watched the world blur past. He thought about the meaning of service.

It wasn't always grand or visible. Sometimes it was simple — listening without judgement, offering a smile to someone unseen, showing up when others withdrew.

The Imam's prayers revealed something subtle: service begins in intention.

Even when the hands cannot act, the heart can still serve by wishing good for another.

"O Lord, make me one whose heart holds mercy for all creation."

He repeated the line quietly, feeling it stretch the boundaries of his self-centred world.

4 · The Modern Mirror

Across from him sat a woman reading a letter, tears in her eyes. He didn't know her story — maybe loss, maybe longing — but he felt moved to whisper a small, silent prayer:

"O God, ease her pain, give her comfort, and send her someone to listen."

He began to look around the carriage differently now — each face a verse in its own story. The tired man in the corner, the student half-asleep on her backpack, the young couple holding hands in nervous silence.

So many worlds, all hidden behind quiet eyes. And suddenly, prayer felt larger — not something confined to words, but an awareness that connected him to everyone around him.

5 · The Voice of the Imam — Friendship and Nearness

He opened his phone and scrolled through old messages — friends he hadn't spoken to in months, maybe years. People who had once been constants, now only memories.

He thought of Imam Sajjad's prayer for friends:

"O God, bless my companions.

Reward those who guided me kindly, forgive those who wronged me gently.

Let my love for them be pure, and my counsel to them sincere.

Gather us in Your remembrance, and draw us nearer to You through one another."

The Imam prayed not only for his friends' success, but for their spiritual well-being — that love itself be sanctified through sincerity.

He smiled, typing a simple message to an old friend: *"Been thinking of you. Hope you're doing okay."* It wasn't much, but it carried warmth.

6 · The Whisper of the Imam

That evening, walking home, he recited softly under his breath:

"O Lord, let my heart be a home for the pain of others, and my hands an answer to their prayers.

Let me serve not for recognition, but for Your sake alone.

And when I forget to pray for others, remind me that I, too, live by the prayers of the unseen."

He thought of his parents, teachers, strangers — people who might once have whispered his name in their duʿāʾ without him ever knowing.

Perhaps that was how the world kept turning — a web of unseen prayers holding everything together.

7 · The Modern Whisper

"O God, when I cannot help, let me still pray.

When I cannot heal, let me still hope.

When I cannot fix the world, let me not grow numb to it. Teach me that prayer itself is action, and compassion is its echo."

8 · Reflection for the Reader

This week, think of three people who cross your mind — maybe those who helped you, those who hurt you, or those you barely know.

Write their names down.

Whisper: *"O God, grant them peace, light, and guidance."*

No one needs to hear it. You'll feel its echo anyway — because every prayer that leaves your lips in sincerity returns to you in mercy.

And if you can, do one quiet act of kindness this week that no one will see — a small service between you and your Lord alone.

That is the Imam's way.

9 · Closing Reflection

The Voice of Service in Imam Sajjad's duʿās teaches us that prayer is not meant to isolate us in holiness, but to connect us in compassion.

When you pray for another, you are transformed — the self softens, pride dissolves, mercy flows.

He shows that even in captivity, even in weakness, a heart that prays for others is never imprisoned.

And so, each time you whisper a name other than your own, you follow in his footsteps — healing the world quietly, one prayer at a time.

CHAPTER TWELVE:
PURPOSE AND PATH

Based on Duʿāʾ 5 and 20:
Seeking Guidance and Light of the Heart

1 · The Crossroads

It was the evening before graduation. The ceremony gown hung on the back of the chair, its folds heavy with expectation.

He stood by the window, staring out at the faint city lights, his reflection merging with the skyline — young, capable, uncertain.

Everyone around him seemed to know their next step. Some were off to jobs, others to postgraduate studies or travel plans. But he felt lost.

"What's my path?" he whispered under his breath. The question carried more weight than he'd expected.

For months, he'd prayed for a sign — a clear answer, a direction. But all he seemed to find was silence.

He opened the worn copy of As-Sahīfa al-Kāmilah al-Sajjādiyyah his grandfather had given him. It fell open naturally to a page that had clearly been read many times. At the top, in careful script, it read: **Duʿāʾ 5 — Seeking Guidance.**

2 · The Voice of the Imam — Seeking Guidance

The words felt alive:

"O God, guide me to the path You love most, and keep my steps firm in Your obedience.

Make my intention pure, my vision clear, and my choices pleasing to You."

He closed his eyes, reading the words again — slower this time.

The Imam wasn't asking for a detailed plan, a map, or a guaranteed outcome. He was asking for clarity of heart.

Maybe guidance wasn't about knowing where to go — maybe it was about trusting where to stand.

The real path, he realised, doesn't begin in front of you. It begins within you.

3 · The Search for Direction

He sat on his bed, letting the stillness of the moment sink in.

He thought about how often he'd treated life like a race — how he'd measured progress by comparison, and purpose by productivity.

But the Imam's words carried a different rhythm — one of patience, surrender, and sincerity.

"O Lord, make me among those whose hearts You have directed toward Yourself, and whose steps You have set upon Your straight path."

He looked up at the faint reflection of himself in the window — the same person, yet not quite. The uncertainty hadn't vanished, but it no longer felt suffocating.

He didn't need to know the whole road. He only needed to see the next step, and to take it with faith.

4 · The Modern Mirror

The next morning, he walked along the canal near his university. The water was still, mirroring the grey clouds.

He thought of his parents' sacrifices, his teachers' advice, the quiet encouragement of friends. All these voices, each with good intentions, had crowded his own.

But now, in the silence, he began to hear something else — the quiet intuition that perhaps, purpose isn't found at all. It's formed.

Every act done with sincerity, every moment lived with awareness, builds the path beneath your feet.

He remembered the Imam's line from *Duʿāʾ 20:*

"O God, illuminate my heart with the light of certainty, until it sees nothing but You in every direction."

He whispered it softly to the water. The reflection trembled, then stilled again — as if the world itself was listening.

5 · The Voice of the Imam — Light of the Heart

Later that day, sitting in the university courtyard, he reread the full passage:

"O God, light my heart with Your guidance.

Strengthen my resolve with Your remembrance.

Protect me from confusion in the face of choices, and from pride when success comes easily.

Teach me that every direction leads to You, if I walk it with sincerity."

He smiled quietly. This wasn't the voice of someone demanding answers — it was the prayer of one who walks in trust.

6 · The Whisper of the Imam

That night, as he prepared for the ceremony, he wrote a small note and placed it in his pocket — a reminder he could reach for in moments of doubt:

"Let every path I take be a way to You, and every delay a lesson in patience."

He didn't know yet what tomorrow would bring — but for the first time, he wasn't afraid of not knowing.

7 · The Modern Whisper

"O God, I do not ask to know my future — only to trust You in it.

If You open a door, let me walk through it with gratitude. If You close one, let me wait with grace.

And wherever I end up, let me be of service, and at peace."

8 · Reflection for the Reader

Pause for a moment.

Think about the question that's been circling in your heart — the decision, the uncertainty, the path you're unsure of.

Now ask yourself, *"Why do I seek it?"*

Is it to be seen, or to be sincere? To impress, or to serve? To prove something to yourself, or to draw nearer to your Lord?

The Imam teaches that clarity is not the same as certainty — it is peace in the midst of uncertainty.

Write down one sentence beginning with:

"O God, guide me toward..." Let it be your whispered map.

9 · Closing Reflection

In the quiet after all the celebrations, he stood again beneath the night sky. The city shimmered below — lights like stars scattered across earth.

He breathed deeply and smiled. He still didn't have all the answers. But he had something far more precious — trust.

Imam Zayn al-ʿĀbidīn's (A.S) Purpose and Path teaches that true direction is not about reaching a destination, but walking with devotion.

Every moment of confusion is a chance to deepen surrender. Every act done with sincerity is a prayer in motion.

And every seeker who whispers,

"Guide me," is already halfway home.

Whispers of the Heart

CHAPTER THIRTEEN:
JUSTICE AND RESPONSIBILITY

Based on Duʿāʾ 23 and the Treatise on Rights

1 · The Wallet

It was raining — the kind of quiet, persistent drizzle that turns pavements into mirrors. He walked home from work, head down, jacket zipped, lost in the blur of lights and thoughts.

That's when he saw it — a small black wallet lying on the curb. He hesitated, looked around. The street was empty.

He picked it up, wiped the rain from its surface, and opened it under the glow of a lamppost.

Inside were a few folded notes, some credit cards, a driving licence. He checked the address on the ID — it was just a few blocks away.

He stood there for a moment, feeling something stir inside him — not greed, exactly, but temptation. After all, no one had seen him. It was late. The owner might never know.

He took a breath. Then another. The rain fell harder, washing the hesitation away.

He closed the wallet, slipped it into his pocket, and began walking toward the address on the ID.

2 · The Voice of the Imam — Responsibility and Faith

As he walked, the rain tapping softly on his hood, a memory surfaced — words he had once read from As-Sahīfa al-Kāmilah:

"O God, guide me to act with justice in all dealings, to honour every trust placed in me, and to stand firm for what is right even when it costs me."

The rhythm of the rain seemed to fall in time with those lines.

He remembered how Imam Zayn al-ʿĀbidīn (A.S) prayed not for wealth or success, but for trustworthiness.

Justice, for the Imam, wasn't just a social ideal — it was a form of devotion. A person who breaks trust, he taught, has fractured something far deeper than law — they've cracked the mirror of their own soul.

He gripped the wallet tighter.

3 · The Weight of Small Choices

When we think of justice, we imagine grand courts, public battles, mighty decisions that shake nations.

But Imam Sajjad reminds us: true justice begins in the smallest places — the moments no one else sees.

A returned wallet. An honest report. A kind word instead of a cruel one.

Those are the quiet tests of faith.

"O Lord, make me fair in hidden things as I strive to be in what is seen."

He reached the address — a small brick house with ivy climbing the side. He rang the bell.

A tired-looking man answered, confusion turning into relief. "Thank you," he said, voice trembling. "I didn't even know I'd lost it."

The man tried to press a note of gratitude into his hand, but he shook his head and smiled. "It's fine. It's yours."

He turned to leave before the man could insist. The rain had eased, and though his clothes were damp, his heart felt strangely light.

4 · The Modern Mirror

Walking home again, he thought about how easy it is to blur the lines between right and wrong — how small compromises pile up, how modern life excuses little acts of self-gain.

He remembered the Imam's Treatise on Rights:

"Know the right of your fellow human being — that you wish for him what you wish for yourself, and never wrong him as you would not wish to be wronged."

Those words cut through the noise of modern excuses. Justice wasn't about appearances. It was about remembering that every action affects someone else — seen or unseen.

He realised that the greatest test of faith is not prayer when others are watching, but integrity when no one is.

5 · The Voice of the Imam — The Web of Responsibility

Later that night, he read another passage from the *Treatise on Rights:*

"Your wealth has a right — to be earned lawfully and spent rightly.

Your neighbour has a right — to be treated with peace and respect.

Your words have a right — to speak truth and not wound.

And your soul has a right — to be purified from deceit."

He looked around his quiet apartment — the mug half-empty on the table, the faint hum of the heater.

He thought of all the invisible rights surrounding him — his co-workers, his family, even strangers on the street. The Imam's words turned daily life into sacred space.

Responsibility, he realised, was not a burden. It was belonging.

6 · The Whisper of the Imam

He whispered softly before sleeping:

"O God,

let my hands be honest, my words fair, and my heart clean in every transaction.

Protect me from deceiving myself when I justify small wrongs.

Let me be a servant of justice even when no one applauds, even when no one sees."

The room fell silent, but his heart felt steady — anchored by something eternal.

7 · The Modern Whisper

"O God, make me brave enough to be truthful, and gentle enough to be just.

Keep me upright in temptation, humble in authority, patient in the face of unfairness.

Let my fairness be my faith."

8 · Reflection for the Reader

This week, reflect:

When was the last time you faced a small moral choice — and chose the harder, honest path?

Where in your life could you act with a little more integrity, fairness, or compassion?

Write it down. Then whisper the Imam's words:

"O God, guide me to act with justice in all dealings."

Remember — justice begins in the unseen.

9 · Closing Reflection

The *Justice and Responsibility* of Imam Zayn al-ʿĀbidīn (A.S) is not about politics or judgment — it's about purity.

He teaches that every believer is a trustee — of truth, of compassion, of fairness. Each small act of honesty becomes a prayer written in action.

He reminds us that there is no such thing as a private virtue. Integrity, like light, always shines outward.

And perhaps that is what justice truly is — not a system, but a state of the soul.

So when the rain falls again, and another quiet choice presents itself, remember the Imam's voice:

"Stand firm for what is right, even when no one sees you — for God always does."

CHAPTER FOURTEEN:
LEADERSHIP AND TRUST

Based on Duʿāʾ 48:
For the Guardians of the People

1 · The Chair at the Table

The meeting room was silent, except for the soft hum of the projector. He sat at the end of the long table, hands clasped, trying to steady his breath.

This was the first time he'd chaired a meeting as manager. Just a few weeks ago, he'd been sitting on the other side — one among many — watching someone else make the calls, take the heat, carry the weight.

Now that someone was him.

He'd thought leadership would feel empowering. Instead, it felt heavy.

Every decision seemed to ripple outward — affecting teams, budgets, futures. Every word carried weight.

As he looked around the table — faces waiting, pens ready — he wondered, *how do you lead without losing yourself?*

2 · The Voice of the Imam — For Those Who Govern

Later that night, he opened his phone, searching for peace in the only place he knew — the words of the Imam.

He found *Duʿā' 48: For the Guardians of the People*.

"O God, guide those who hold authority among Your servants.

Let their hearts be filled with mercy, their actions with justice, and their words with truth.

Strengthen them to uphold what is right, and protect them from pride that blinds."

He read it again and again.

The Imam didn't ask for rulers to be feared — he asked for them to be merciful. He didn't pray for their power — he prayed for their humility.

And he didn't limit this prayer to kings or governors. He spoke to every soul that holds influence — in a home, a classroom, a workplace.

Leadership, the Imam taught, is not a privilege. It's a test.

3 · The Weight of Responsibility

He remembered something his mentor had told him:

"Leadership is not about being in charge. It's about being accountable."

But accountability is heavy. It means standing in the open, shouldering not just your choices — but their consequences.

He thought about how easy it would be to misuse authority: to protect his image instead of his team, to stay silent when honesty might offend, to prioritise comfort over conscience. And then he remembered the Imam's words:

"O Lord, let not the fear of people make them neglect Your justice. And let not the love of power distract them from the truth."

The words cut through him. He wasn't a ruler of nations — but in small ways, he governed too.

How he led mattered. How he treated those below him mattered even more.

4 · The Modern Mirror

The next morning, he faced his first real test.

A mistake had been made in a project. His team waited nervously for his response. It wasn't his fault — but it had happened under his leadership.

He could shift the blame, or he could own it.

He remembered the Imam's *Du'ā'*:

"O God, let those entrusted with others be guardians, not tyrants; caretakers, not exploiters."

He took a deep breath.

"This one's on me," he said.

"We'll fix it together."

The room relaxed — not because the problem vanished, but because trust was built.

That night, walking home under the glow of the streetlights, he realised something profound: leadership wasn't about control — it was about conscience.

5 · The Voice of the Imam — Trust and Humility

That evening, he read further in the Imam's prayer:

"O God, bless those who guide others.

Protect them from greed that corrupts, and from arrogance that deceives.

Remind them that they govern souls, not possessions, and that every decision will be weighed in Your scales."

He paused. The Imam's words carried both tenderness and warning.

True authority, he realised, is sacred. It can lift or destroy. And the higher one stands, the more humility is needed.

He looked back at his day — the small decisions, the quiet moments, the unspoken influence. All of it was part of a trust.

6 · The Whisper of the Imam

Before sleeping, he whispered softly:

"O Lord, make me a leader only if I can serve.

When I rise, let me rise with honesty. When I fall, let me fall with grace.

Let my influence heal, not harm.

And never let me forget that every decision writes my character in the book only You will read."

7 · The Modern Whisper

"O God, let my voice carry fairness, not fear.

Let my silence never enable wrong.

Give me the courage to correct myself before correcting others.

Teach me that every title fades, but every act of mercy remains."

8 · Reflection for the Reader

This week, reflect:

Who do you influence — directly or quietly?

How can you lead with gentleness instead of authority?

How can you make your words feel like shelter, not command?

Write down one sentence that begins with:

"O God, let my leadership..." and complete it honestly.

Leadership is not limited to status; it lives in every act of guidance, every moment of example.

9 · Closing Reflection

Imam Zayn al-ʿĀbidīn's (A.S) Leadership and Trust transforms power into prayer. He redefines strength as humility, and authority as servanthood.

For him, to govern even one person — a child, a student, a community — is to bear a sacred trust.

The Imam prays not for dominance, but for integrity in influence. He teaches that the true leader is not the one who commands obedience, but the one who awakens conscience.

And in a world that often mistakes pride for confidence, his words return us to the essence of leadership:

"Power is a trust, not a triumph."

So whether you sit at the head of a table, or simply guide one heart — remember: your authority is temporary, but your impact is eternal.

CHAPTER FIFTEEN:
NATURE AND THE ELEMENTS

Based on Duʿāʾ 46 and 35:
For Rain and For Morning and Evening

1 · The Rain After Silence

The afternoon had been long and loud. Emails, traffic, screens — everything demanded his attention. But as he stepped out of the office that evening, the sky broke open.

Rain began to fall — not violently, but softly, a thousand drops tapping the roofs, pavements, and faces of the rushing crowd.

He hesitated at the doorway. Everyone else ran for cover — under bus shelters, coffee shop awnings, heads bent against the drizzle.

He stayed where he was.

For the first time that day, no one asked anything of him. The rain fell without expectation, without needing to be noticed — yet it renewed everything it touched.

He closed his eyes and let a few drops fall on his face. And somewhere deep inside, a verse rose like breath:

"O God, pour upon us the rain of Your mercy, revive the deadness of the earth and the dryness of our hearts."

It was from Duʿāʾ 46 — the Prayer for Rain.

He had read it before, but standing there now, the words felt real.

The Imam's world was alive — each raindrop a messenger of renewal.

2 · The Voice of the Imam — For Rain

He opened his phone and found the passage again:

"O God, send down upon us the rain of benefit, the blessing of abundance, not of harm or hardship.

Let it descend upon the plains and the mountains, the earth and the trees, until every thirsty soul and leaf praises You anew."

The Imam didn't see weather as a random event — he saw it as revelation. Each natural element — wind, cloud, seed — was a verse in the book of creation.

He remembered how the Imam lived through hardship, captivity, and scarcity, yet his prayers overflowed with gratitude for the earth's signs.

Perhaps the secret of his peace was this:

when you see everything as God's speech, you can find meaning in every storm.

3 · The Breath of Creation

He began to walk, slowly, watching the puddles shimmer under the streetlights.

How strange, he thought — how this same rain that ruined plans also revived the world. How easily we forget that what seems inconvenient may be mercy in disguise.

In As-Sahīfa, the Imam spoke of this rhythm constantly — that every act of creation is worship.

"Glory be to You, O Lord, whose praise is sung by the thunder in its fear, and whose glory the lightning declares in its obedience."

The mountains submit by standing still, the rivers by flowing freely, the trees by bowing when the wind commands.

Every atom, every creature, is remembering.

He realised: maybe remembrance doesn't mean reciting aloud — maybe it means existing truthfully, just as God intended.

4 · The Modern Mirror

A few days later, he decided to wake early. The city was still half-asleep when he reached the park. Mist hovered over the grass; a single bird called from a tree.

He sat on a bench, breathing in the cold, clean air.

The sunrise began slowly — first a faint blush of gold, then a sudden flood of warmth, as if the heavens themselves exhaled light.

He felt something shift inside — a peace that no achievement had ever given him.

He remembered *Duʿāʾ 35:*

"O God, with the morning, awaken my gratitude; with the night, forgive my heedlessness.

Grant me the blessing of another day, so that I may remember You in it."

The Imam's dawn was not merely a time of day — it was a moment of awakening.

Morning was for gratitude. Evening was for forgiveness. And everything in between was for remembrance.

5 · The Voice of the Imam — Morning and Evening

Later, reading by the window, he came across another line:

"O God, this new morning has appeared, and every creation of Yours stands ready to obey You.

The heavens rise by Your command, the winds blow by Your mercy,

the earth yields its gifts by Your generosity, and I stand before You — seeking my portion of guidance and grace." He paused, letting the words linger.

The Imam's universe was not mechanical — it was intimate. Creation wasn't something outside to be observed; it was something alive to be joined in worship.

He thought about how disconnected the modern world had become — how screens had replaced skies, how progress had muffled wonder.

And yet, even now, the wind still moved in obedience, the sun still rose in gratitude. The only silence came from human forgetfulness.

6 · The Whisper of the Imam

That night, as he lay by the window, the moonlight spilling across the floor, he whispered softly:

"O Lord, let me rise with the dawn in praise, and rest at dusk in peace.

Teach me to see Your signs in every breeze, and Your mercy in every drop.

When I walk upon the earth, let it be with reverence.

When I drink from its water, let it be with gratitude.

For all of creation is prostrate before You — let me not be the one who forgets."

7 · The Modern Whisper

"O God, let every sunrise be a lesson, and every sunset a remembrance.

When the rain falls, remind me to soften my heart. When the wind blows, remind me to let go. When the trees bow, remind me to be humble.

And when the stars appear, remind me how small I am — and how loved."

8 · Reflection for the Reader

Take a moment this week to walk outdoors — not with music in your ears, but with awareness in your breath.

Look at the light as it changes, listen to the rustle of leaves, notice how even stillness is movement in disguise.

Then whisper the Imam's words:

"O God, awaken my gratitude with the morning."

Try writing about one moment in nature that felt sacred — even if it lasted only a second. Describe how it reminded you of something divine.

9 · Closing Reflection

In Nature and the Elements, Imam Zayn al-ʿĀbidīn (A.S) teaches that creation is not merely scenery — it is scripture written in colour, wind, and water.

To watch the rain, to feel the dawn, is to witness the world praying.

He reminds us that nature does not need us to speak for it — it already remembers its Lord perfectly. We are the ones in need of remembering.

So the next time you hear thunder, imagine it saying SubḥānAllah. The next time you see rain, let it wash your heart before the ground.

Because, as the Imam whispers through every element:

"The earth itself remembers its Creator — will you?"

CHAPTER SIXTEEN:
TIME AND TURNING POINTS

*Based on Duʿāʾ 44–45 and 31:
Ramadan and the End of the Year*

1 · The Clock That Stopped

The power went out just after midnight. The house fell silent — the hum of the fridge faded, the screen went black, and in the sudden darkness, even time seemed to pause.

He looked up at the clock on the wall. Its second hand had frozen mid-tick.

For the first time in a long while, there was no noise, no light, no movement — just quiet. He sat there, waiting for something to resume.

It didn't.

And in that stillness, he noticed something:

the silence wasn't empty.

It was alive.

It was the sound of everything that kept moving even when we stopped — breath, heartbeat, thought, prayer.

He whispered, almost involuntarily,

"O God, You are the Master of time, the One through whom all beginnings begin and to whom all endings return."

He didn't know it then, but that was how Imam Zayn al-ʿĀbidīn (A.S) often began his reflections — by pausing.

2 · The Voice of the Imam — The Coming of Ramadan

When the lights came back on, he opened his worn copy of *As-Sahīfa al-Kāmilah al-Sajjādiyyah*. The ribbon marker was placed on Duʿāʾ 44 – For the Coming of Ramadan.

"O God, this is the month You have exalted, the time You have chosen, and the season You have made a field of mercy."

He read the words slowly. To the Imam, time was not a series of passing moments — it was a spiritual landscape. Each season carried an invitation, each month a message, each day a hidden purpose.

The Imam did not fear time; he befriended it. He spoke to it, welcomed it, and honoured its passing like one honours a beloved guest.

3 · The Turning of Time

He remembered the feeling of the first night of Ramadan — the quiet expectancy, the soft glow of lamps, the way hunger turned into reflection, and silence into prayer.

How different that time felt — not rushed, not filled with noise or demands. Everything slowed into meaning.

The Imam described Ramadan not merely as a month, but as a living presence:

"Peace be upon you, O month of patience,

O companion of days and nights,

you have purified the hearts of the faithful

and brought near those who seek nearness."

It struck him then — Ramadan wasn't only a span of thirty days. It was a rhythm of remembrance — a reminder that the soul, too, moves in cycles of hunger and fulfilment, absence and return.

4 · The Modern Mirror

When Ramadan ended, he felt the same emptiness the Imam had described in Duʿāʾ 45 - Bidding Farewell to Ramadan:

"Peace be upon you, O month that softened our hardness, and taught our tongues to remember.

You came to us gentle, and you depart leaving us changed."

He closed the book and stared out the window. Outside, the streetlights flickered; the night was deep and still. He remembered how quickly things fade — seasons, people, routines, ambitions. The world moved in cycles, but his heart often resisted.

We crave permanence, yet everything around us teaches the opposite: the flower blooms and wilts, the child grows, the year ends, the loved one departs.

He thought — maybe time is not meant to be held. Maybe it's meant to be heard. Every passing moment whispering, *"Don't cling — become."*

5 · The Voice of the Imam — The End of the Year

As another year approached its close, he turned to Duʿāʾ 31 - For the End of the Year.

"O God, this is the year's end, in which You have kept us in safety and blessed us with provision.

And now we stand before a door of renewal — between what has passed and what is to come."

He paused over the word door. That was how the Imam saw time — not a wall, but a passage. Every ending was an entrance into something greater.

"O God, forgive us for what the year carried of forgetfulness, and accept what it held of goodness.

Bless the coming one with Your mercy, and let its mornings begin in remembrance of You."

He smiled. The Imam's prayers were not simply for forgiveness — they were for continuity. To him, life wasn't a series of disconnected moments; it was a conversation with God that never truly ended.

6 · The Whisper of the Imam

That night, he whispered into the quiet:

"O Lord, let me not count my days by work or worry, but by remembrance and mercy.

Let each sunrise be a promise, each sunset a reflection.

When I waste time, forgive me. When I value it, bless me.

And when my days run out, let my last breath be a beginning — not an end."

7 · The Modern Whisper

"O God, teach me to begin again when I fail, and to end well when I succeed.

Let me meet every change with gratitude, and every loss with grace.

Make me unafraid of time, for it is Yours — and so am I."

8 · Reflection for the Reader

This week, pause.

Find one moment of transition — a birthday, a deadline, a new season, a goodbye. Instead of rushing through it, honour it.

Ask yourself:

What has this season taught me?

What am I being invited to release?

What deserves to continue into the next chapter of my life?

Then whisper the Imam's prayer:

"O God, bless what remains of my time as You blessed what has passed."

Time is not your enemy; it is your teacher. And the one who listens to time learns the rhythm of divine mercy.

9 · Closing Reflection

In Time and Turning Points, Imam Zayn al-'Ābidīn (A.S) transforms the passage of time into an act of worship. He teaches that beginnings and endings are not opposites — they are mirrors.

Ramadan arrives to awaken, departs to refine, and time itself becomes the pulse of remembrance.

When we live heedlessly, time becomes a thief. But when we live consciously, time becomes a companion — one that ushers us gently toward the Eternal.

Every breath, every dawn, every farewell is an invitation to rediscover the One who never changes.

So when the clock stops, and the room grows silent again, remember:

it is not silence —

it is God's reminder that eternity is already unfolding.

"Every ending," the Imam reminds, "is a disguised beginning — and every moment is a door to mercy."

CHAPTER SEVENTEEN:
THE HEART THAT LOVES

Based on the Whispered Prayer of the Lovers
(Munājāt al-Muḥibbīn)

1 · The Empty Room

The house was quiet. Too quiet.

He had spent the evening cleaning, sorting, deleting old messages, trying to silence the echo of something that had ended — a friendship, a chapter, perhaps even a version of himself.

But no amount of order could calm the ache that lingered. It wasn't loud — it was steady, like the heartbeat that you only hear when the world stops speaking.

He sat on the floor of his empty room, the lamp casting a dim pool of light around him.

He didn't want to pray, but he opened his worn book anyway — As-Sahīfa al-Kāmilah al-Sajjādiyyah.

The page that unfolded read:

"The Whispered Prayer of the Lovers."

He almost closed it again. The word lovers felt too tender, too human. But something in him stayed still. He began to read.

2 · The Voice of the Imam — The Prayer of the Lovers

"O God, who made the hearts of Your lovers delight in Your remembrance, who made the spirits of those who yearn for You long for Your meeting,

how can I find rest apart from You?"

The words entered the silence like light entering water. They didn't explain — they transformed.

The Imam spoke of love not as emotion, but as awareness. To love God was to recognise that even pain was His language. Every longing was a form of remembrance, every ache a sign of presence.

He realised: this restlessness he felt — this aching void — wasn't punishment. It was invitation.

3 · The Meaning of Divine Love

He sat there, eyes still on the page, and began to understand what love meant in the Imam's world.

Love was not about possession. It was about purification.

It burned away illusions, leaving only what was true. It stripped the heart of its false gods — pride, fear, self-importance — so that it could finally bow in freedom.

"My God," the Imam whispered, "who can taste the sweetness of

Your love and seek another?"

He thought about all the people and things he had chased — career, approval, affection, stability — and how quickly they faded.

But the moments of sincerity, of quiet tears, of being broken and still choosing to hope — those remained.

Perhaps that was divine love: to keep searching even in the dark, trusting that every absence is actually a form of calling.

4 · The Modern Mirror

Outside, the night deepened. He remembered another time — a loss that had shattered him so completely he'd sworn he would never feel again.

But now, sitting here, he saw how even that heartbreak had been a teacher.

It had humbled him.

It had softened him enough to pray.

The Imam's words returned:

"You are the delight of the hearts of Your lovers,

the goal of the seekers,

the companion of those who remember You."

He closed his eyes. Tears came, quiet and without drama. For once, they felt clean — not heavy with regret, but gentle, like something being released.

Maybe love was not about being understood by others, but about being unveiled before God — and realising you were never unloved, even when you were unseen.

5 · The Voice of the Imam — The Cry of Longing

He read further, the voice of the Imam trembling with both awe and intimacy:

"O Lord, when will the hearts of Your lovers rest in Your nearness?

When will their eyes be cooled by Your sight?

When will the clouds of separation lift, and the sun of closeness rise?"

He could almost hear it — the yearning of a soul that had seen both love and loss, and understood that distance is only meaningful because closeness exists.

The Imam wasn't asking for paradise; he was asking for presence. He wanted not reward, but relationship.

And that was when it struck him — to love God is to be brave enough to be vulnerable before Him.

6 · The Whisper of the Imam

He whispered softly, echoing the Imam's rhythm:

"O God,

let my longing for You outlast every longing.

Let my nearness to You be my home.

Make my heart restless until it rests in You, and my tears a path that leads only to Your mercy."

The room felt less empty now.

It wasn't filled with sound — but with a quiet warmth that words couldn't name.

7 · **The Modern Whisper**

"O God,

teach me to love You in silence, to seek You in patience, to recognise You in every reflection of kindness.

When I fall in love with the world, let it be only because it reminds me of You.

And when I lose what I love, let me remember that You remain."

He looked up, and for the first time in a while, he smiled — not because the ache was gone, but because it finally made sense.

8 · **Reflection for the Reader**

Pause here.

Think of a moment in your life when love — in any form — transformed you. Maybe through beauty, maybe through loss.

Ask yourself:

What did that experience teach you about God?

Write it down — not as a story, but as a whisper.

Then close your eyes and repeat:

"O Lord, You are the one who made my heart capable of love — let it return to You purified by it."

Remember:

Every feeling of love is a shadow of divine tenderness. Every longing is a form of prayer.

9 · Closing Reflection

In The Heart That Loves, Imam Zayn al-ʿĀbidīn (A.S) reveals that divine love is not found in grand gestures, but in stillness, patience, and sincerity.

To him, the lover's highest joy is not in being loved, but in loving.

When we seek God not for reward, but for relationship, worship becomes intimacy.

Every sigh becomes dhikr. Every tear becomes a testimony. Every silence becomes a meeting place.

Love, he teaches, is not a journey toward God — it is the discovery that He was already within the journey all along.

So when your heart aches, when longing feels too much to bear, remember the Imam's whisper:

"My God, You are the light of the eyes of those who love You, the comfort of the hearts of those who yearn for You, and the closeness of those who seek You."

And in that realisation — you will find the sweetest form of nearness.

CHAPTER EIGHTEEN:
HOPE AND DOUBT

Based on the Whispered Prayer of the Hopeful and Duʿāʾ 47 (For Nearness to God)

1 · The Grey Morning

The morning light slipped through the curtains, pale and tired. He sat at the edge of the bed, staring at the mug of tea cooling beside him. Nothing was wrong, yet everything felt muted — as if colour itself had taken a day off.

He tried to pray, but the words felt mechanical. He opened his mouth, then closed it again. The same verses that once carried meaning now felt far away, like echoes in a language he couldn't quite recall.

He whispered softly,

"Why does the heart go quiet when I need it to speak?"

He didn't know it, but the Imam had asked the same question centuries ago.

2 · The Voice of the Imam — The Prayer of the Hopeful

He reached for his worn copy of As-Sahīfa al-Kāmilah al-Sajjādiyyah and opened it at random — as if asking the book itself to guide him.

The page read:

The Whispered Prayer of the Hopeful — Munājāt al-Rāji'īn.

He began to read aloud, slowly:

"O God, if You do not accept me for my deeds, then accept me for my hope in You.

If You turn me away for my sins, then grant me refuge in Your mercy."

He stopped. The words felt as if they had been written for this exact morning.

Even the Imam — the great grandson of the Prophet, a man of devotion and knowledge — had moments when he spoke not from strength, but from yearning.

It wasn't perfection that connected him to God; it was persistence.

3 · The Valley of Doubt

He thought about how often faith is painted as certainty — clear, unwavering, radiant. But the Imam's words showed something gentler, and perhaps truer.

Faith isn't the absence of doubt. It is walking through doubt with your eyes open.

There are days when belief feels effortless — and days when even hope feels heavy. Yet the Imam whispers:

"O Lord, though my deeds weigh me down, my trust in Your mercy lifts me up."

He closed the book and sat in silence. The line echoed in his chest. Maybe it wasn't about feeling close to God — maybe it was about staying turned toward Him, even when you felt far away.

4 · The Modern Mirror

Later that day, he sat on a park bench watching people pass. The air was crisp; the trees stood bare and patient. He thought about seasons — how they all serve their purpose.

Spring blooms, summer thrives, autumn releases, winter rests. Even in nature, silence and emptiness aren't failure — they are preparation.

Maybe the heart works the same way. Maybe doubt isn't a void, but a season between understanding and renewal.

He remembered a line from his grandmother's notebook: "God sometimes hides in silence so that we may learn to call louder."

He smiled faintly — it made sense now.

5 · The Voice of the Imam — The Anchor of Mercy

That night, he returned to his reading.

He found *Duʿāʾ* 47 — For Nearness to God:
"O God,
make my certainty stronger than my doubts,
my hope greater than my fear,
and my trust firmer than my anxiety."

He whispered the words slowly, as if building a bridge back to peace.

The Imam didn't pray to erase his fear — he prayed to balance it. Faith, he taught, is not light without shadow; it's learning how to walk through both.

6 · The Whisper of the Imam

"O Lord,

when I feel lost, remind me that even my search is guided.

When I am afraid, let me remember that fear, too, leads me to You.

When I fall silent, listen to what my heart is trying to say."

He felt something loosen inside him. Not a sudden rush of clarity, but a small quiet — like the first warm breeze after a long winter.

7 · The Modern Whisper

"O God,

let my heart break only to let Your light in.

Let me question without despairing, and hope without demanding.

Teach me to trust the process of becoming — the slow, unseen miracle of Your timing."

He exhaled deeply. The fog hadn't disappeared, but he could see a soft outline of light through it.

Maybe that was all faith needed — not answers, just a direction.

8 · Reflection for the Reader

Pause for a moment.

Think of a time when you were uncertain — when life felt silent, when God felt far.

Now ask yourself: Did something eventually emerge from that silence — a lesson, a strength, a new path?

Write it down. Name that moment not as loss, but as light delayed.

Then whisper the Imam's words:

"O God, if You turn me away for my deeds, then accept me for my hope in You."

Because every moment of doubt is a door through which hope learns to walk.

9 · Closing Reflection

In *Hope and Doubt*, Imam Zayn al-ʿĀbidīn (A.S) teaches that spiritual life is not a straight line — it's a rhythm of closeness and distance, of breaking and mending, of silence and speech.

Hope is not born in comfort. It grows in the soil of uncertainty. It is the soul's quiet defiance — the refusal to give up on mercy.

He reminds us that the heart's journey is not measured by how often it shines, but by how it returns to light when it dims.

So when you find yourself between belief and confusion, remember the Imam's whisper:

"Even when I am far, You are near. And even when I forget, You still remember."

And that is the essence of hope — the certainty that the light is never gone; it is only waiting for you to look again.

Whispers of the Heart

CHAPTER NINETEEN:
THE WORLD AND CREATION

Based on Du'ā' 23 and Du'ā' 27:
For the People of the Frontiers and For the Believers

1 · The Newsfeed

The screen lit up in the dark. Headline after headline scrolled past — wars, hunger, floods, children with faces covered in dust. He scrolled faster, as if speed could protect him from the weight of it all.

He wasn't numb; he was overwhelmed. What could one prayer, one heart, one person possibly do in a world this broken?

He closed the app, placed the phone down, and stared at the ceiling. The silence that followed was thick — a kind of ache. He wanted to care, but he didn't know how anymore.

That was when he remembered Imam Zayn al-'Ābidīn (A.S) — the man who had survived a massacre, captivity, and loss, and yet somehow still prayed for others.

He opened *As-Sahīfa al-Kāmilah al-Sajjādiyyah*. The page that met him read:

"For the People of the Frontiers."

2 · The Voice of the Imam — For the People of the Frontiers

"O God,

strengthen the protectors of the borders of Your lands.

Make their hearts gentle toward the weak, their hands firm against injustice, and their intentions pure for Your sake." He read it twice.

It wasn't just a prayer for warriors — it was a prayer for anyone who stands at the edge of something fragile: those defending peace, those protecting truth, those carrying hope where the world has grown cold.

The Imam's prayer wasn't about power. It was about mercy.

Even in times of war and vulnerability, he prayed that strength never lose compassion.

And he realised — the "frontier" the Imam spoke of might not just be geographical. It could be the moral frontiers of our time: between greed and generosity, apathy and empathy, fear and faith.

3 · The World as One Breath

He looked out the window. The streetlights hummed. Somewhere far away, other people were looking out their windows too — each carrying their own unseen weight.

It struck him then — humanity was not a collection of individuals. It was a single organism breathing in many rhythms.

When one heart breaks, the rest of the world quietly feels the tremor. When one person prays sincerely, it softens a thousand unseen hearts.

That was the Imam's vision — a spiritual ecology where

compassion is contagious.

"O God," the Imam wrote, "fill the hearts of the faithful with gentleness, link their souls together in harmony, and make their hands open in goodness toward one another."

This was not utopia. It was moral realism — a faith that begins with empathy.

4 · The Modern Mirror

He remembered a time when prayer felt small — when the world's suffering seemed too vast to touch.

But now he saw that the point was not to fix everything. It was to remain human in a world that forgets how.

He thought of how Imam Sajjad prayed not only for friends, but for strangers, enemies, travellers, the poor, the ill, and even animals. No one was left out of his mercy.

His faith had no borders. His duʿāʾs were the language of universal kinship.

He whispered to himself,

Maybe I cannot heal the world.

But I can refuse to harden my heart against it.

5 · The Voice of the Imam — For the Believers

He turned the page to Duʿāʾ 27 – For the Believers.

"O God, forgive all believing men and women, link their hearts together, unite their paths toward goodness, and make the end of their deeds better than the beginning."

He paused at the phrase link their hearts together.

The Imam prayed not for individual salvation, but for collective harmony. He understood that faith is never private. It breathes through community.

"O Lord," the Imam continued, "grant safety to the frightened, health to the sick, return to the traveller, and forgiveness to the deceased."

Every verse carried someone else's story. Every word was empathy translated into prayer.

And he thought — perhaps the truest way to love God is to love everything He created.

6 · The Whisper of the Imam

He placed the book down and whispered:

"O Lord,

let my heart be too wide for hatred, too alive for indifference.

When I see suffering, let compassion move me faster than despair.

When I see beauty, let gratitude follow before envy.

Teach me to pray not only for what I need, but for what the world needs."

The silence that followed was different now — not heavy, but sacred.

It felt like the quiet after rain — the kind where the earth listens.

7 · The Modern Whisper

"O God,

let my compassion travel farther than my voice.

When I pray for peace, make it begin with me.

When I pray for justice, make me just.

When I pray for mercy, teach me how to forgive."

He realised then that prayer was not about escape — it was about engagement. It was not turning away from the world, but turning toward it through God.

8 · Reflection for the Reader

Pause.

Think of one person or group you've never met — someone far away who suffers or struggles.

Now imagine their life for a moment. Their air, their sky, their fears, their joys.

Then whisper:

"O God, bless them as You bless me.

Relieve their pain as You have relieved mine."

You may not see the change, but something will soften — in them, and within you.

Because every sincere prayer for others is also a healing for the heart that prays.

9 · Closing Reflection

In *The World and Creation,*

Imam Zayn al-ʿĀbidīn (A.S) reminds us that faith is not confinement — it is expansion. Prayer is not retreat — it is return.

He teaches that creation itself is a shared duʿāʾ. The oceans, winds, and stars — all whisper His name. And humanity, in its diversity and struggle, is meant to echo that chorus in its own way.

When you pray for another, you are remembering that you belong to them — and they to you.

So let your duʿāʾs be wide, your mercy borderless, your heart large enough for the world.

Because the Imam's voice still calls across the centuries:

"O God, unite the hearts of Your servants,

let peace descend where there is division,

and let Your remembrance fill every corner of the earth."

And perhaps that is the greatest prayer of all — not for escape from the world, but for its awakening.

CHAPTER TWENTY:
THE BEAUTY OF WORSHIP

Based on the Whispered Prayer of the Worshippers and

the Duʿāʾ of the Night

1 · The Quiet Mosque

The mosque was almost empty. Only a handful of people remained — their silhouettes still in the soft amber light. The sound of a distant clock echoed through the hall, marking time that no one here seemed to follow.

He had come without expectation. It had been a long, noisy day — messages, meetings, chatter. He had prayed earlier, quickly, words running faster than meaning.

But something had drawn him back tonight — a quiet pull, like a whisper saying, *"Be still. Listen."*

He sat against the cool wall of the mosque. No one was speaking,

but the silence itself seemed alive — as if the air carried the weight of unspoken devotion.

He thought:

maybe this is what worship really sounds like — not noise, not movement, but awareness.

2 · The Voice of the Imam — The Prayer of the Worshippers

He opened As-Sahīfa al-Kāmilah al-Sajjādiyyah to a passage marked long ago.

The title read:

The Whispered Prayer of the Worshippers — Munājāt al-ʿĀbidīn (AS).

He began to read softly:

"My God, You are the companion of those who remember You,

the solace of those who find peace in You,

the friend of those who worship You sincerely.

You are the light of the hearts of those who love You,

and the comfort of the souls of those who long for You."

He paused after every line, as though the words themselves were alive, breathing in the pauses between them.

The Imam didn't speak about worship as obligation. He spoke about it as friendship — as intimacy between Creator and creation.

He wasn't describing ritual; he was describing relationship.

3 · The Still Heart

He thought about all the times he had rushed through prayer —

the times when his lips moved but his heart was somewhere else. When salah became checklist, not conversation.

The Imam's words were an invitation back to presence. Every breath, every bow, every moment of stillness was a chance to say,

"I am here, my Lord — and You are here too."

He remembered reading once that Imam Zayn al-ʿĀbidīn (A.S) would tremble when he performed ablution, saying, *"Do you not know before whom I am about to stand?"*

It wasn't fear — it was love so deep it made him humble.

Perhaps that's what true worship feels like: not performance, but presence. Not perfection, but participation.

4 · The Modern Mirror

He looked around the mosque again — a young man praying slowly, an elderly man lost in quiet remembrance, a woman with her hands raised, eyes closed in stillness.

Each was speaking a different language, yet the silence bound them together.

He thought about how modern life has trained us to be everywhere except here — to think of tomorrow while standing in today. And yet, the Imam's way of worship was the opposite — to anchor the soul in the now.

He whispered to himself:

Maybe worship isn't about saying more;

maybe it's about meaning more.

5 · The Voice of the Imam — The Night Prayer

He turned to another passage — The Duʿāʾ of the Night. The Imam's voice here felt different — softer, almost like a lullaby.

"O God, how can I sleep while You watch over me?

How can I forget when You never forget me?

My waking is in Your mercy, my sleeping in Your care, and my heart in Your remembrance."

He imagined the Imam at night — alone, eyes lifted toward the stars, each prayer a whisper into the vastness.

Night, for him, wasn't emptiness. It was audience. It was meeting the One who listens without reply, but always responds.

He closed his eyes and breathed. The mosque lights dimmed as the last worshipper left. He stayed behind, letting the stillness settle around him like a cloak.

6 · The Whisper of the Imam

He whispered softly, echoing the tone of the Imam's prayer:

"O Lord, when I bow, let my heart bow too.

When I stand, let it be in humility.

When I am silent, let my silence speak.

Let me worship not only with limbs, but with longing.

Let my prayer be less about words and more about witnessing."

He realised — worship was not only an act done to God, it was something done with Him.

A meeting, not a performance.

7 · The Modern Whisper

"O God, teach me to pray not to be seen, but to see You.

When distraction pulls me, pull me back with love.

When words fail, let the rhythm of my heart complete the prayer.

When I have nothing to say, let my silence be enough."

He felt lighter, as though every unspoken prayer of his life had been heard in that moment.

8 · Reflection for the Reader

Find one moment of stillness this week.

No music, no screens, no requests — just presence.

Sit quietly. Breathe deeply. Let your thoughts slow until you can hear your own heartbeat.

Then whisper to yourself,

"O God, You are here."

That's worship. Not the words — the awareness.

Every moment can become prayer when the soul remembers who it belongs to.

9 · Closing Reflection

In The Beauty of Worship, Imam Zayn al-ʿĀbidīn (A.S) teaches that devotion is not a burden, but a blessing.

He reveals that the truest form of prayer is not when we speak, but when we listen — to the silence between our words, to the presence within our breath.

He transforms worship into intimacy — a rhythm of love, stillness, and gratitude.

When the world moves too fast, his whispered duʿāʾs remind us that every heartbeat is a place of meeting.

"O Lord," the Imam teaches, "let me not grow weary of standing before You, for in standing before You I find my rest."

And that is the paradox of worship:

it tires the body, but it rests the soul.

In silence, you find sound. In stillness, you find movement. In prayer, you find presence — the quiet miracle of being seen, and loved, by the One who never sleeps.

CHAPTER TWENTY-ONE:
THE TRAVELLER'S PATH

Based on the Duʿāʾ for the Traveller and Duʿāʾ for Protection

1 · The Station Platform

The station was quiet at dawn. Only the sound of footsteps, rolling suitcases, and the soft hiss of trains breathing mist into the cold morning air.

He stood on the platform, half-awake, watching the sky slowly change from grey to amber. Around him, people were leaving — some hugging goodbyes, others lost in headphones and thoughts. Each carried a story, a reason, a destination.

He felt the familiar ache of departure — that small ache that comes from knowing every beginning hides a farewell inside it.

As the whistle blew and the train began to move, he whispered instinctively:

"O God, accompany me in this journey."

He didn't know where the words came from. But when he checked his small notebook later, he found them written exactly as Imam Zayn al-ʿĀbidīn (A.S) had once prayed.

2 · The Voice of the Imam — For the Traveller

"O God,

accompany us in our journey,

protect us from its hardships,

guard us from its fears,

and return us home safe and rewarded.

You are the Companion in travel,

and the Guardian of the stay."

He read those words softly, his voice nearly drowned by the rumble of the train.

The Imam didn't just pray for safety — he prayed for presence. His journey was not just through deserts or valleys; it was through the landscape of the soul.

To him, travel was not merely movement. It was trust.

And in those few lines, he had given the map: travel with awareness, walk with humility, return with gratitude.

3 · The Inner Journey

He stared out of the window — fields blurred into horizon, villages passed like fleeting dreams.

How much of life, he thought, is like this train ride?

You move constantly, yet sit still. You pass by so much beauty, but see only a fraction of it.

He realised that every physical journey mirrors an inner one. The heart, too, travels — from ignorance to awareness, from fear to faith, from self to surrender.

"O God," the Imam whispered in another prayer,

"You are the one who guides the lost traveller,

and brings the stranger back home."

Maybe, he thought, the real journey was not outward at all — it was the long walk back to the self that trusts God again.

4 · The Modern Mirror

He remembered his first time leaving home — how heavy the suitcase had felt, not because of its weight, but because of the life he was leaving behind.

He thought about all the roads since then — airports, highways, crowded buses, unfamiliar rooms — each teaching something about faith.

The Imam's words returned to him:

"You are the Companion in travel."

He smiled. Even when he'd travelled alone, he'd never been truly alone.

Every coincidence that had protected him — every delay that saved him, every kindness from a stranger, every unseen detour — perhaps they weren't random after all.

Maybe divine companionship wasn't about visions or voices, but about being carried through the day without knowing how.

5 · The Voice of the Imam — For Protection

That night, he arrived in a quiet town. The streets were empty, lit by orange lamps. As he unpacked, he opened the Sahīfa again —

this time to the Duʿāʾ for Protection.

"O Lord, be my guardian in this journey,

my shelter in fear,

my comfort in loneliness.

Keep me safe from what I cannot see,

and guide my steps toward what You have decreed with wisdom."

He read slowly, his eyes filling with calm. The Imam prayed not only for protection from danger — but from despair.

Even in the unknown, he asked for inner security — the kind that cannot be taken by distance or loss.

And as the wind whispered outside his window, he realised something profound: Faith doesn't remove uncertainty.

It redefines it.

It turns every risk into relationship.

6 · The Whisper of the Imam

"O Lord, wherever I go, You are my destination.

In every road, You are the path.

In every delay, You are the wisdom.

In every return, You are the welcome."

He closed the book. The quiet of the room felt full — not empty, but accompanied.

7 · The Modern Whisper

"O God, make every road a reminder that nothing in life is wasted if travelled with You.

When I am far from home, let Your nearness be my comfort.

When I lose my way, let remembrance guide me back.

And when I arrive, let gratitude be the first thing I unpack."

He thought of all the people constantly moving — migrants, students, pilgrims, seekers. Each on a different road, yet all walking the same invisible journey: toward return.

8 · Reflection for the Reader

Think of a journey that changed you — not because of where you went, but because of who you became.

Was it a trip, a move, a moment of loss, a new beginning?

Now ask:

Who protected me in the spaces between?

What unseen hands guided me back when I didn't even know I was lost?

Then whisper the Imam's words:

"You are the Companion in travel,

and the Guardian of the stay."

Every step you've taken — even the wrong ones — were part of the road that leads you home.

9 · Closing Reflection

In The Traveller's Path, Imam Zayn al-ʿĀbidīn (A.S) teaches that every movement in life is sacred when begun with remembrance.

Journeys are not measured by distance, but by awareness — how often we turn to God along the way.

When the Imam prayed, he didn't ask for the road to be easy — he asked for the heart to remain steady.

Because the true traveller doesn't just move from place to place — they move from self to soul, from distraction to devotion.

He reminds us that life itself is a journey of return — a long road back to the One who first sent us forth.

"O God," the Imam whispers,

"when I leave, protect me.

When I return, receive me.

And when I reach the end of all roads,

let it be to You."

CHAPTER TWENTY-TWO:
THE POWER OF WORDS

Based on Duʿāʾ 47 and the Treatise on Rights

1 · The Conversation That Went Too Far

It had started as a small joke. Something said in passing, half in laughter, half in pride. But the words hung in the air longer than he intended. He noticed the look on the other person's face — the way their smile faded, how they fell quiet.

Later that night, as he replayed the moment in his mind, the regret settled in. He wanted to take the words back — but words, once released, rarely return.

He thought of the Imam's teaching — that every word is a winged thing: once it leaves your tongue, it takes flight toward its consequence.

He opened As-Sahīfa al-Kāmilah al-Sajjādiyyah and turned to Duʿāʾ 47 – For Good Manners and Noble Character.

2 · The Voice of the Imam — For Good Manners

"O God, adorn me with the garment of the righteous, and clothe me with the beauty of the humble.

Let me speak only when my words add to goodness, and be silent when silence is wiser."

He read the passage slowly, feeling the weight of its simplicity.

The Imam did not separate worship from conduct. For him, prayer without character was a shadow without light.

In every line, he was asking not only for guidance, but for gentleness —

that his words might become doors of mercy, not weapons of pride.

He paused and whispered:

"O God, teach me to speak as if every word is being recorded in eternity."

3 · The Right of the Tongue

He turned to the Treatise on Rights, a document the Imam had written outlining over fifty human and spiritual responsibilities.

Among them was one that always struck him — *The Right of the Tongue.*

"And the right of the tongue is that you should consider it too noble for obscenity, accustom it to good speech, and discipline it with silence — except when benefit is to be gained."

He read those lines again and again. The Imam was not forbidding speech — he was refining it. He understood that the tongue reveals what the heart hides.

Every insult is a confession. Every kindness is a mirror.

The words we speak create the atmosphere in which our souls breathe. To guard the tongue, therefore, is to protect the climate of the heart.

4 · The Modern Mirror

He thought about the world now — how easily words spill across screens. How quickly opinions become weapons. How often silence is mistaken for weakness, and shouting for truth.

He remembered times when he had typed out anger and pressed send too soon, when sarcasm felt easier than sincerity.

And he thought of how the Imam lived in a time of political unrest, surrounded by cruelty and deceit — yet he never raised his voice to wound, only to awaken.

He whispered, half to himself, *Maybe true strength isn't in saying more, but in saying what matters most.*

5 · The Voice of the Imam — The Virtue of Restraint

He read further in Duʿāʾ 47:

"O God, give me a tongue that remembers You often, a heart humbled before You, and a soul content with what You decree. Guard me from words that lead to regret, and from speech that wounds even in jest."

He paused at the phrase "speech that wounds even in jest."

How subtle the Imam's understanding was — he knew that cruelty often hides behind laughter, and arrogance behind eloquence.

For him, restraint was not repression. It was refinement. He prayed for a tongue so truthful, it could only speak what healed.

6 · The Whisper of the Imam

He whispered softly, letting the words sink like rain into quiet soil:

"O Lord, let my words heal, not harm.

Let my silence be my wisdom when anger calls.

Let my speech be soft when others are harsh, and my truth gentle even when it must be firm.

Teach me to remember that the ear of Heaven hears before the ear of man."

The air around him felt lighter. It wasn't the kind of peace that erased regret — it was the kind that promised transformation.

He realised that remorse, too, is a kind of mercy. It reopens the heart's gate to humility.

7 · The Modern Whisper

"O God, make my voice soft in disagreement,

and my words truthful in solitude.

When I am tempted to prove myself,

remind me that silence is sometimes the proof of faith.

When I speak, let it be with purpose.

When I am silent, let it be with patience."

He smiled. The same tongue that could wound could also bless. And the same silence that could hide fear could become an act of reverence.

8 · Reflection for the Reader

Think back to a conversation that stayed with you — maybe because it hurt, or maybe because it healed.

What made those words powerful? Tone? Intention? Timing? Truth?

Now imagine your words as seeds. What would grow in the hearts of those who hear them?

The Imam teaches that every word is a prayer in disguise. It either builds bridges or burns them.

So before you speak, ask: *Will this draw me — and them — closer to God?*

If not, silence is the better sentence.

9 · Closing Reflection

In *The Power of Words,*

Imam Zayn al-ʿĀbidīn (A.S) reveals that language is not neutral — it is sacred. To speak is to shape reality. To listen is to honour creation.

He teaches that humility in speech is not weakness; it is wisdom dressed as gentleness.

In his world, good manners (makārim al-akhlāq) were not politeness for its own sake, but the reflection of a purified soul.

He reminds us that the tongue is both pen and mirror — it writes our character and reveals our truth.

"O God," the Imam prays,

"beautify my tongue with truth, and my heart with sincerity.

Let my words rise like fragrance — and fall like mercy."

When you next speak, imagine your words as guests leaving your lips — will they travel with grace, or return carrying regret?

That awareness — that sacred pause between impulse and expression — is where character lives.

CHAPTER TWENTY-THREE:
THE LANTERN OF LEARNING

Based on Duʿāʾ 20, Duʿāʾ 23, Duʿāʾ 47, and the Treatise on Rights

1 · The Library Light

The library was half-empty. A faint hum of computers, a scatter of open books, and the soft rustle of pages filled the night. He sat beneath the dim yellow lamp, highlighters around him like small stars. His eyes ached from study, yet something deeper in him felt tired — not of work, but of why.

He stared at the words on the page and whispered under his breath, *"I'm learning so much, yet I don't feel any closer to meaning."*

The sentence hung in the air, as if waiting for an answer. He opened a small notebook he carried — a place where he wrote reflections, prayers, and pieces of his faith journey. Inside, he had once copied a passage from As-Sahīfa al-Kāmilah al-Sajjādiyyah.

He found it now — written in fading ink:

"O God, grant me understanding that leads to obedience, and a heart that holds Your remembrance."

He read it slowly, line by line. It was from **Duʿāʾ 23 — For Knowledge and Understanding.** And in that moment, the line felt alive.

2 · The Voice of the Imam — For Knowledge and Understanding

"O God, teach me knowledge that benefits me, and keep me from learning that brings pride.

Illuminate my sight with truth, and let my heart become a lamp of understanding."

For Imam Zayn al-ʿĀbidīn (A.S), knowledge was never just information. It was a light meant to purify — not to glorify. He saw learning as a form of worship, and the student as a servant of both truth and humility.

He never separated intellect from intention. In his worldview, to know was to draw nearer to God — not to rise above others.

The library around him felt different now. Each book looked less like an object, and more like a door. What if every fact, every line, every discovery, was simply another way of learning more about the One who created all things?

3 · The Light of the Heart

He thought about how the Imam called knowledge "nūr al-qalb" — the **light of the heart**. Light doesn't boast; it simply shines. It doesn't compete with darkness; it transforms it.

Perhaps that was the meaning of study: not to build walls of superiority, but to scatter light into confusion and ignorance.

He remembered the Imam's words in Duʿāʾ 20 - Light of the Heart:

"O God, fill my heart with light,

and make my tongue the guide of truth.

Open within me the doors of wisdom,

and close upon me the gates of ignorance."

He closed his eyes and imagined a lantern inside his chest — flickering softly. Every act of sincere learning, every moment of wonder, was like adding oil to that flame.

4 · The Modern Mirror

He thought about all the pressure he felt — exams, expectations, future plans. Sometimes it seemed like life had turned knowledge into currency rather than clarity. Grades became trophies, not gateways.

He smiled bitterly — how easy it is to chase recognition and forget revelation.

And yet, when he remembered the Imam's prayer, something shifted. He realised the goal was not to know more, but to know better — to know with humility, to understand with purpose.

He whispered to himself:

"Maybe real education is when learning changes who you are, not just what you can do."

5 · The Voice of the Imam — The Teacher and the Student

He turned the pages of Risālat al-Ḥuqūq — the Treatise on Rights, where the Imam described over fifty responsibilities every believer holds.

He found two that spoke directly to him: **the Right of the Teacher and the Right of the Student.**

"The right of your teacher is to honour him as the one who guides you to wisdom. Do not argue with him, nor raise your voice above his. Respect him as a messenger from God."

"And the right of your student is to teach him with mercy,

to guide him without pride,

and to be patient with his questions,

for he is the seeker of the truth you hold."

He thought of his professors, mentors, and even his parents — how often he had forgotten that teaching is a sacred trust, and learning a form of gratitude.

Knowledge, in the Imam's world, was not ownership — it was stewardship.

6 · The Whisper of the Imam

He whispered softly, letting the words become prayer:

"O Lord, let my learning make me humble, not proud;

useful, not loud.

Let my curiosity lead to compassion,

my ambition to service,

and my success to gratitude.

If I forget the purpose of knowledge,

remind me that all truth returns to You."

He felt the heaviness lift. It wasn't that his work got easier — but his why became clearer.

7 · The Modern Whisper

He wrote a short note to himself in his notebook:

"Don't just chase answers — chase understanding.

Don't just learn for applause — learn for awakening.

Every book you open, open your heart beside it.

The greatest degree is to graduate from ignorance to awareness."

He smiled — a small, quiet smile of realisation. Maybe the Imam's lessons weren't only for the scholars and saints. They were for anyone who wanted to learn how to live wisely, and how to serve beautifully.

8 · Reflection for the Reader

Think of something you're learning right now — a subject, a skill, a lesson life is teaching you.

Ask yourself:

Is it making you kinder?

More aware?

More grateful?

If not, what would happen if you studied it through the lens of intention? Could your learning become worship — a way of serving others and drawing nearer to truth?

Pause and whisper:

"O God, make my knowledge light,

and my heart its lantern."

9 · Closing Reflection

In *The Lantern of Learning,* Imam Zayn al-ʿĀbidīn (A.S) teaches that knowledge without humility is darkness disguised as brilliance. True learning is not measured by mastery, but by the gentleness it leaves behind.

He shows that youth is not an age of confusion — it is an age of becoming: when the mind questions, and the soul begins to listen.

For him, the classroom was not a place of ego, but a prayer hall of reflection.

"O God," the Imam prays, "increase me in knowledge that brings me close to You, and keep me from knowledge that distracts me from Your path."

And so the student closed his books that night — not with exhaustion, but with peace. The lamp above flickered, mirroring the lantern now burning within his chest.

He realised then what the Imam had always known: to learn is to awaken, and to teach is to light another flame.

CHAPTER TWENTY-FOUR:
THE RETURN

Based on Duʿāʾ 31 (At the Time of Death) and the Whispered Prayer of the Thankful

1 · The Final Sunset

The horizon was a blaze of gold fading into amber, the kind of sunset that holds you still. He watched the light slowly withdraw from the sky, the world growing quieter with each minute.

It felt like a gentle rehearsal for farewell — the sun setting as if to remind him that even endings can be beautiful.

He thought of the countless days he had lived, how many dawns he had woken to, how many nights he had survived. Each one a small mercy he had taken for granted.

Now, in the soft twilight, a question rose in his heart: *What would it mean to be ready?*

He opened *As-Sahīfa al-Kāmilah al-Sajjādiyyah,* turning to a page he had rarely read aloud before — the **Duʿāʾ at the Time of Death**.

2 · The Voice of the Imam — For the Time of Death

"O God,

make my death a release from every sorrow,

and my meeting with You the joy of my eyes.

Purify my soul before it returns to You,

and let my final breath carry Your name."

He read the lines slowly. There was no fear in the Imam's words — only familiarity, as though he were speaking of a journey already known to the heart.

To him, death was not darkness. It was a homecoming.

Every duʿāʾ he had ever whispered had been preparing him for this moment — to walk through the final door with peace, not panic.

3 · The Meaning of Return

He reflected on the Arabic word the Imam used — rujūʿ — return.

It was such a gentle word. Not ending, not loss, not disappearance. Return.

Like the river returning to the sea. Like the flame returning to its source of light. Like a child returning to a mother's embrace.

The Imam saw life as a loan from God, and death as its repayment — not out of obligation, but gratitude.

He whispered,

"You sent me into the world to know You — and now I return to see You."

In that sentence, fear dissolved.

4 · The Modern Mirror

He thought of the hospital corridors he had walked, the funerals he had attended, the silence of gravesides broken only by sobs.

He remembered the first time he lost someone — how the room felt suddenly empty, how the ordinary objects they left behind became sacred.

Back then, he could not make sense of it. But now, reading the Imam's words, he saw it differently.

Those who leave are not erased — they are gathered. Those who die are not gone — they have gone ahead.

And when he remembered their laughter, their kindness, their patience, he realised they had already taught him how to die — by teaching him how to live gently.

5 · The Voice of the Imam — The Thankful Heart

He turned to the *Whispered Prayer of the Thankful (Munājāt al-Shākirīn)*. If death frightened the world, the Imam met it with gratitude.

"My God,

if You withhold, I will still praise You,

for withholding from You is giving.

If You afflict, I will still thank You,

for affliction from You is mercy.

How can I not be grateful,

when every breath is a gift from Your compassion?"

He paused, eyes moist.

It was strange — the Imam was facing mortality, yet spoke with joy. He didn't ask for escape; he asked for awareness.

Gratitude, he realised, was not the opposite of pain. It was the transformation of it.

6 · The Whisper of the Imam

He closed the book and whispered softly, words half prayer, half surrender:

"O Lord,

when the time comes for my return,

let my final breath be a sigh of gratitude, not of fear.

Let my heart recognise the road home.

Let me see familiar mercy waiting in the light.

And if my deeds fall short,

let Your forgiveness complete the rest."

He sat in the fading light until night took the horizon. The stars appeared — countless, calm, as though watching over him in quiet affirmation.

7 · The Modern Whisper

He wrote a few lines in his journal, as if to leave a note for the self he would one day become:

"O God, when my time comes,

let me meet You with a heart unafraid, and eyes that recognise where they are going. Let those I love be left with peace, not questions.

Let me return to You as one who has finally found home."

He smiled faintly — not out of courage, but out of trust.

8 · Reflection for the Reader

Death often feels like a shadow we refuse to name. But Imam Sajjad turns it into a mirror — not to terrify, but to teach.

Ask yourself gently: If today were my last day, what would I want to carry with me?

Regret or remembrance?

Complaint or gratitude?

Make a list — not of possessions, but of mercies. Moments that shaped you, faces that softened you, prayers that saved you quietly.

That list is your preparation — because gratitude is the soul's passport home.

9 · Closing Reflection

In *The Return,*

Imam Zayn al-'Ābidīn (A.S) teaches that the story of life is written in a single circle — from God, to God.

He shows that peace is not found by avoiding death, but by understanding it.

The believer's final journey is not a departure; it is a reunion with the Source of all love.

"O God," the Imam prays,

"when my soul is drawn back to You,

let it return like a bird that finds its nest.

Let my ending be a beginning,

my silence a hymn,

and my dust a remembrance."

He looked out once more at the horizon. The night was vast, the stars countless. And yet, he felt utterly seen — small in body, infinite in belonging.

He whispered the final words before closing his notebook:

"From You we came.

To You we return.

And between those two mercies —

we live, we learn, we love."

And somewhere, in the unseen, the voice of the Imam seemed to echo softly:

"Peace be upon those who return in gratitude."

Glossary of Key Spiritual Terms

Dua — A personal supplication; the act of calling upon God with sincerity and honesty.

Sahifa — Literally "record" or "scroll"; the title of Imam Zayn al-Abidin's (AS) collection of supplications.

Imam Zayn al-Abidin (AS) — The fourth Imam from the family of the Prophet, known for his humility, patience, and eloquence in prayer.

Tawba — Repentance; the journey of returning to God after mistakes or forgetfulness.

Sabr — Patience and steadfastness in times of trial.

Shukr — Gratitude; recognising and thanking God for blessings, both seen and unseen.

Rizq — Sustenance and provision; what God grants us for both body and spirit.

Tawakkul — Trust and reliance upon God while striving with effort and sincerity.

Dhikr — Remembrance; keeping awareness of God alive through reflection and repetition.

Ilm — Knowledge, both intellectual and spiritual.

Nafs — The self or inner being that struggles between good and weakness.

Rahma — Mercy and compassion that surround every aspect of creation.

Husayn ibn Ali — Grandson of the Prophet and father of Imam Zayn al-Abidin (AS), whose sacrifice at Karbala shaped the Imam's spiritual outlook.

Risalat al-Huquq — The "Treatise on Rights," a moral guide by the Imam describing duties owed to God, the self, and others.

Munajat — A whispered prayer; an intimate conversation with God.

Akhlaq — Character and moral conduct.

Fitrah — The pure spiritual nature with which every human being is created.

Marifah — Deep spiritual recognition of God's presence.

Rujoo — The soul's return to its divine origin.

EPILOGUE — THE CIRCLE OF LIGHT

*A Journey of the Soul through the Duʿās of
Imam Zayn al-ʿĀbidīn (A.S)*

It began, as all journeys do, with a whisper.

A whisper that said: *"There is more to this breath than survival."*

From that whisper, awareness was born — a moment of awakening, a realisation that behind every heartbeat stands the Giver of hearts.

The journey began in **praise** — in awe of the One who sustains all things, the One who listens before we even call.

And then it moved — slowly, painfully — through the valleys of the self. Through guilt, repentance, struggle, patience. Through nights when the only prayer was tears, and mornings when gratitude felt like rebirth.

Every stage in this book, every duʿāʾ, was a mirror. A reflection of what it means to be human, and a reminder of how mercy meets us exactly there.

The Arc of the Journey

In **awareness**, the soul learned to notice.

In **repentance**, it learned to soften.

In **gratitude,** it learned to see.

In **service,** it learned to give.

In **silence,** it learned to listen.

And in love, it learned to dissolve the boundaries between self and surrender.

Through **family,** it found compassion.

Through **society,** it found connection.

Through **knowledge,** it found light.

Through **worship,** it found peace.

And through **death,** it found home.

This is the circle of the Imam's teaching — not a line that ends, but a spiral that returns, again and again, to its Source.

The Voice of the Imam

"O God,

I praise You not because I understand You,

but because I have seen Your mercy

in everything I do not understand."

Imam Zayn al-ʿĀbidīn's (A.S) duʿās were not composed from comfort. They were written from captivity, loss, and the ruins of Karbala. And yet, they are filled not with despair, but with tenderness.

He turned grief into gratitude.

He turned isolation into intimacy.

He turned silence into dialogue with the Divine.

Every page of the *Sahīfa* is a map — not to escape the world, but to walk through it with awareness.

The Modern Heart

You, the reader, carry the same questions that his prayers once answered:

How do I find peace in pain?

How do I forgive when I'm wounded?

How do I trust what I cannot see?

How do I make my life a prayer?

The Imam's voice still answers — not with philosophy, but with presence.

He reminds you that spirituality is not somewhere else. It is here — in every breath, every decision, every word spoken with sincerity.

The Whisper of the Imam

"My God,

the hearts of Your friends are windows of light.

Through their gratitude, others learn to see.

Through their patience, others learn to hope.

Through their worship, the world learns stillness."

His prayers are still teaching, still reaching across centuries, still lighting lamps in the dark.

And perhaps that is the purpose of reading them — not only to understand, but to become what we read.

The Modern Whisper

"O Lord,

I am not yet what I wish to be,

but every time I turn to You,

I am less of what I was.

Let my life be a long return,

my heart a lantern of remembrance,

my silence a place where Your voice lives."

The Return

At the end of all prayers, there is only one prayer left: *gratitude*.

For to thank God is to finally recognise the pattern — that everything was mercy disguised as mystery.

The journey ends where it began — in the awareness of presence. In the breath of surrender. In the whisper of love.

"From You we came.

To You we return.

Every step in between

is a step toward home."

Final Reflection

When you close this book, may you not leave the Imam's voice behind. Let it echo in your mornings and your pauses, in your decisions and your silences.

Let every act of kindness be a duʿāʾ, every challenge a chapter, every moment an opening.

Because *As-Sahīfa al-Kāmilah al-Sajjādiyyah* is not only a book of prayers. It is a conversation — between you, the world, and the One who never stopped listening.

And now, as the final page turns, the circle closes:

Awareness becomes gratitude. Gratitude becomes peace. Peace becomes return.

And return — becomes reunion.

"Peace be upon those

who remember their Lord,

in the beginning,

in the middle,

and in the end."

Whispers of the Heart

ACKNOWLEDGEMENTS

This book ends as it began — in gratitude.

To those who kept the light of *As-Sahīfa al-Kāmilah al-Sajjādiyyah* alive through centuries of devotion and remembrance, your faith is the bridge between the Imam's whisper and our world today.

To the hearts who read, reflected, and shared — thank you for turning these words into lived prayer. Each moment of reflection, each quiet breath of remembrance, is a continuation of this journey.

To the families, teachers, and companions who nurture stillness and sincerity in a world that often forgets both — your presence is a form of worship.

And above all, to the One who guided the pen, and turned doubt into direction, and silence into speech — Alhamdulillah.

May this work be accepted as a small offering of love and remembrance, and may it lead every reader closer to the Light from which all words begin.

Whispers of the Heart

Index of Duas Referenced in This Book

This index links each section of The Sahifa of the Heart to the corresponding supplications found in As-Sahifa al-Kamilah al-Sajjadiyya, allowing readers to explore the original prayers alongside the reflections.

1 — The Call to Awareness

Draws from Dua 1 (Praise of God) and Dua 5 (Seeking Guidance). It also echoes the Whispered Prayer of the Worshippers.

2 — The Mirror of the Soul

Inspired by Dua 12 (Confession of Sins) and Dua 20 (Light of the Heart).

3 — The Weight of Wrong

Reflects on Dua 16 (Seeking Pardon) and the Whispered Prayer of the Repenters.

4 — The Quiet Battle

Based on Dua 7 (Hardship) and Dua 14 (Seeking Refuge), with themes drawn from the Whispered Prayer of the Fearful.

5 — The Gift of Gratitude

Centres on Dua 35 (Morning and Evening) and the Whispered Prayer of the Thankful.

6 — The Bonds That Raised Me

Draws from Dua 24 (For Parents), Dua 25 (For Children), and Dua 26 (For Neighbours).

7 — Circles of Trust

Inspired by Dua 27 (For Friends) and Dua 38 (For Neighbours).

8 — Lessons and Learning

Rooted in passages from Dua 23 (For Knowledge and Understanding).

9 — Earning and Enoughness

Draws on Dua 18 (Seeking Provision) and Dua 19 (Against Greed).

10 — Body and Breath

Based on Dua 15 (For Illness) and Dua 6 (For the Sick).

11 — The Voice of Service

Connected to Dua 23 (For the Frontiers of Islam) and Dua 47 (For Nearness to God).

12 — Purpose and Path

Guided by Dua 5 (Seeking Guidance) and Dua 20 (Light of the Heart).

13 — Justice and Responsibility

Reflects Dua 23 (For the People of the Frontiers) and teachings from the Treatise on Rights.

14 — Leadership and Trust

Drawn from Dua 48 (For the Guardians of the People).

15 — Nature and the Elements

Inspired by Dua 46 (For Rain) and Dua 35 (Morning and Evening).

16 — Time and Turning Points

Based on Dua 44 and 45 (Prayers for Ramadan and its Farewell) and Dua 31 (At the End of the Year).

17 — The Heart That Loves

Built around the Whispered Prayer of the Lovers.

18 — Hope and Doubt

Draws from the Whispered Prayer of the Hopeful and Dua 47.

19 — The World and Creation

Rooted in Dua 23 (For the Frontiers) and Dua 27 (For Believers).

20 — The Beauty of Worship

Echoes the Whispered Prayer of the Worshippers and the Dua of the Night Vigil.

21 — The Traveller's Path

Refers to the prayer For Travelling and Protection.

22 — The Power of Words

Linked with Dua 47 (For Noble Character — Makarim al-Akhlaq) and the Treatise on Rights.

23 — The Lantern of Learning

Draws from Dua 20 (Light of the Heart), Dua 23 (For Knowledge), and Dua 47 (For Good Manners).

24 — The Return

Refers to Dua 31 (At the Time of Death) and the Whispered Prayer of the Thankful.

Whispers of the Heart

Closing Note

All dua numbers correspond to the standard compilation of *As-Sahifa al-Kamilah al-Sajjadiyya*.

Readers are warmly encouraged to return to the original supplications — in translation or Arabic — to deepen reflection and experience the prayers in their complete form.

Whispers of the Heart

www.ingramcontent.com/pod-product-compliance
Lightning Source LLC
Chambersburg PA
CBHW052032070526
44584CB00016B/2008